Coyote at the Kitchen Door

Coyote at the Kitchen Door

Living with Wildlife in Suburbia

STEPHEN DeStefano

Harvard University Press

Cambridge, Massachusetts

London, England

2010

Illustrations by Debby Kaspari

Library of Congress Cataloging-in-Publication Data

DeStefano, Stephen, 1956–
Coyote at the kitchen door : living with wildlife in suburbia / Stephen DeStefano.
p.   cm.
Includes bibliographical references and index.
ISBN 978-0-674-03556-0 (alk. paper)
1. Urban animals.   2. Coyote.   3. Urbanization—Environmental aspects.   I. Title.
QH541.5.C6D47   2010
591.75′6—dc22   2009035387

To my parents

Contents

Preface

The issue of urban and suburban development is a popular topic of discussion today for a variety of reasons. Urban and suburban sprawl, as it has been called, and the lifestyle that goes along with it, affect our lives in many different ways.

Any telling of the story of sprawl starts with our use of resources and the tremendous inputs of energy, materials, and services needed to support our way of life. Among the most obvious is our reliance on automobiles. For the past few decades we have worried about our dependency on oil and automobiles and about the problems (for example, air pollution and climate change) that go along with it, but now that oil supplies and gasoline prices are so unpredictable, the issue has come to the forefront in the nation's consciousness. Part of the story of sprawl would have to focus, too, on the way we live: the things we have gained, especially material goods, but also perhaps the things we have lost, such as a closer sense of community. And part of the story has to do with wildlife. The wildlife subplot in the story of sprawl certainly involves the animals that are forced out or killed off by our overwhelming occupation of the landscape. We may not mean to drive them away or cause their deaths, but it happens nonetheless. At the same time, there are animals that seem to do fine or even flourish within our town and city limits. Here is one of the paradoxes that characterize life as we know it: some species continue to show a decline in numbers or a reduction of their geographic range, and may even face the threat of extinction, while other species move right in among us, annoying us, scaring us, and fascinating and pleasing us all at the same time.

As with all matters affecting people, resources, land use, and lifestyles, our relation to wildlife is somewhat complex. I faced these complexities as I wrote, and as a consequence I feel compelled to explain a bit about the structure and content of the book before we get too far into it.

First off, as much as I have tried to base *Coyote at the Kitchen Door* on scientific fact, this is not a science book. Scholarly works written by experts in the field who aim to synthesize the latest findings and facts on a particular scientific topic—including books on urban and suburban wildlife and related issues—are proliferating. That outpouring follows on the heels of an explosion of primary scientific literature in a wide range of peer-reviewed scientific journals, such as the *Journal of Wildlife Management; Conservation Biology; Ecology;* and *Ecological Applications,* that address issues related to urban and suburban wildlife. Entire journals, such as *Urban Ecosystems* and *Human-Wildlife Conflicts,* are now devoted largely to the topic of urban and suburban ecology.

Part of my goal in writing was to try to bring some of the relevant scientific information, as seen through the lens of my own personal and professional experiences, to a wider audience. The scientific community does not really need my perspective on the topic. So many professionals are currently engaged in this arena that one more voice is hardly necessary. Nature is really as much a passion as a profession for me, anyway, and I hope that part of my compassion and concern for wildlife will come across to people who have not really given nature a lot of thought, whose love for the natural world remains largely unfulfilled because of the busyness of their lives, or who may have an active distrust or dislike of nature because of some negative experience.

Second, I never intended for so much of this book to be written in the first person. When organizing the first outline for it, I envisioned a more detached approach to the topic of urban and suburban wildlife. As I wrote, however, the account became more personal. Then when I was partway through my draft, I had a humbling experience. I had been happily working away, making a lot of statements along the lines of "I did this" and "I thought that," when a friend of mine told me he always avoids writing in the first person. He wouldn't feel comfortable writing that way and furthermore thought it was somewhat presumptuous to do so. The conversation brought me up short. If an experienced writer felt this way, who was I to think otherwise?

After that conversation, I spent quite a bit of time thinking about my unconstrained use of the first person, but after a time I realized I was stuck. I *couldn't* write this book in anything *but* the first person. My life and who I am are so tied up with my profession and my feelings about nature that it was impossible to extract or extricate my self from what I wanted to say. The writing had evolved into something even more personal than I'd intended. I still don't want this book to be about me, but I am so mixed up in it all that I can't take myself out of it, either. *Coyote* is an attempt to translate the things I have seen and experienced in suburbia and in the wild into a perspective on where we are going as a society and the world we are leaving behind in our headlong rush toward the successful suburban lifestyle.

Finally, a word about the structure of the book is in order. Each chapter contains three parts: a narrative introduction that focuses on some species of wildlife in a wild place; the central part of the chapter, which addresses an issue related to the urban/suburban environment, and a concluding vignette that describes the life and times of a prominent, adaptable, and often controversial species: the North American coyote.

The lead-in section to each chapter is not necessarily related to the main topic discussed in the chapter, but that is actually not the point. My experiences in the field and my interactions with wild animals in nature seemed to be so different from my experiences in suburbia that I wanted to explore the contrasts and look for any similarities that may exist. I also wanted these brief introductory narratives to provide an opportunity to leave suburbia for a moment, to see what might be happening in other places. How often do any of us have a chance to visit the tundra, hike in the desert, or even walk in the woods close to home? Yet while we are keeping up with our busy lives, wild animals are out there in the world, doing what they do every day, mostly out of our range of vision and our cognizance. When we do get a chance to visit a wild area and see some wildlife, our paths cross briefly. At the end of each encounter we must leave the wild places and wild things to return to the human, developed world in some form. This is the common thread to such encounters, which I have come to call the leaving. It is part of the story that we all share in the lives we have chosen— the great leaving—the turning away from nature for something else, something of our own making. In the main portion of each chapter in *Coyote*, too, we return from the wild to the surroundings, issues, and circumstances that are of our own making.

The story of the coyote presented at the end of each chapter is not necessarily related to the chapter itself either, but it is a quintessential example of the life of an animal taking place right under our noses, as we go to work and school and spend time at home and with our families. The story of the coyote in suburbia is too compelling not to tell, and I am certainly not the first to try to do so, nor will I be the last. The coyote will persist, and its stories will need to be told and retold from time to time, because the coyote is constantly reinventing itself. That is part of the coyote's legacy, and a large part of our tale as Americans.

All these components of this account—my encounters with wild nature, my work, my upbringing in suburbia, and my current, more rural lifestyle—are so tied up together for me that I have never been successful at keeping them separate, and I have come to see that our lives and the lives of wild animals are parallel realities. That perspective brought the book together as I wrote. I hope I've provided a decent synthesis of human development of the environment and its meaning for and impact on both wildlife and people. Mainly, this book is my attempt to face what I believe is the largest conservation issue of our lifetimes. In twenty-five or more years of traveling and working in the northeastern, midwestern, and western United States, parts of Canada and Mexico, and a few other places in the world, I have witnessed our struggles with wildlife management, timber harvest, grazing, crop damage and livestock loss inflicted by wildlife, habitat loss and protection, hunting and antihunting sentiments, endangered species recovery, and water use. All these issues are important, complex, and controversial, but none compares with the proliferation of human beings and the impact of our urban and suburban views of the world. We are now seeing that what we do really does affect the way the earth responds, and like it or not, we are caught up in it. There was a time, in our lifetimes if you are my age or older, when we could pass off the implications of what we were doing to the planet to generations not yet born. We thought, maybe this will have an impact on our grand-children's children. Now I believe we can look into the faces of *our* children to see the ones who will be dealing directly with the consequences of our lifestyle. Everything really is interconnected, and that is more than pretty prose in a series of nature essays. It is all happening right now: this is where we find ourselves in history, and it is everyone's issue—it is a first-person state of affairs.

New Salem, Massachusetts

Coyote at the Kitchen Door

The sky met the earth again, and Coyote came forth.

—Tohono O'odham Creation Story

Prologue

Suburban Beginnings

In the summer of 1970, at the age of fourteen, I thought I had a pretty good idea of what it took to be a wildlife biologist. I formed this opinion from the pages of *National Geographic* magazine. I would sit up in bed after supper and thumb through back issues, rereading the stories and poring over the pictures of John and Frank Craighead studying grizzly bears in Yellowstone National Park, Maurice Hornocker chasing mountain lions through some wilderness valley in central Idaho, or David Mech training his telemetry antenna on an unseen collared wolf in the north woods of Michigan.[1] Outside my window, my third-floor view of the world was very different from Idaho or Isle Royale or Yellowstone. I could hear robins making their final calls on the day, and I knew that a skunk might be patrolling the lawn looking for grubs later in the evening, but the suburbs of Boston were not the place for a wildlife biologist. Wildlife biologists studied wild animals in wild places. Watertown, Massachusetts, was not one of them.

Twelve years later, in the spring of 1982, I became a wildlife biologist. I picked this date to mark my entry into the profession for a couple of reasons: I had just completed an M.S. degree in wildlife ecology and, at about the same time, landed my first paying job as a biologist. Before the ink was dry on the thesis, I was in a van traveling north out of Madison, Wisconsin, for Winnipeg, Manitoba. I had been hired by the Wisconsin Cooperative Wildlife Research Unit, at that time a component of the U.S. Fish and Wildlife Service, to join a small crew of biologists headed to Cape Churchill, Manitoba. The mission was to collect data on Canada geese on their breeding grounds: the density of nests, number of eggs per nest, number of eggs hatched, and size of the resulting broods. Such information was used every year by the U.S. Fish and Wildlife Service, the Canadian Wildlife Service, and the states and provinces in the Mississippi

Flyway to forecast the size of the fall flight of migrating geese, set hunting quotas, prepare for damage to agricultural crops, and otherwise manage the birds as they flew south in the autumn. It was a dream job for a new wildlife biologist.

Yet it really wasn't the new degree or the first job that was the focus of my attention back then on that drive north, but rather my anticipation about the place where I was going for the summer. Cape Churchill is a point in northern Manitoba that juts out from the western shore of Hudson Bay. It is below the Arctic Circle, but because of the effect of the bay the environment is arctic—or more appropriately subarctic—tundra. I knew from pictures that the terrain was basically flat but dotted with countless lakes and ponds, covered in sheetwater in the spring and blanketed with diminutive wildflowers all summer long. The Cape Churchill region comprised hundreds of square miles of wild country on the edge of a bay that stayed frozen most of the year. Snow could, and occasionally did, fall twelve months a year. It didn't look much like Watertown.

Cape Churchill is a breeding ground for Canada geese, snow geese, tundra swans, and dozens of other waterbirds. It is also home to caribou, arctic foxes, wolves, lemmings, and, most famously, polar bears: the big white bears that live on the ice all winter, hunting seals and surviving under incredibly harsh conditions in a forbidding landscape. When the pack ice melts away in late June or July, the bears have nowhere to go but onto the land. The cape is thus a gathering place for hundreds of the great bears, for this is where ice stays longest in the spring and forms first in the fall, allowing the bears greater access to seals. Because of these facts of geography and local climate, the town of Churchill, thirty miles to the west, rightly proclaims itself the "polar bear capital of the world."[2]

In late March 1982, then, we pointed the van northwest and drove out of Wisconsin, across Minnesota, on up through North Dakota and into the province of Manitoba . . . "Friendly Manitoba" as it says on the license plates. In two days' time we were in Thompson and boarding the overnight train to Churchill. What people say about train travel is true—there is really no better way to go. We made our way north, rocking to the constant sway of the train on the rails, being drawn into an adventure by a big locomotive engine that was doing its job somewhere way up ahead. Every so often we could catch a glimpse of the engine from the window when the train moved into a long sweeping curve out of the forest and onto the plains of central Manitoba. The trees grew more sparsely now, and when we awoke the next morning and, from our bunks, peered out the windows in dim light, the trees would all but disappear, and the sign would say, Welcome—*Bienvenue*—to Churchill.

From the airstrip in town it was a short flight out to the cape. We arrived at camp in late April, when snow still lay on the ground, and fell to work. We dug out the Quonset hut that would be our home for the next five months, repaired the buildings, set up the radio and the water system, got a fire going in the oil burner, stocked the shelves and freezer pit with canned goods and fresh meat, and stowed our personal gear and field equipment. We dressed in wool pants, felt-lined leather boots, and balaclavas. In a couple of weeks we would change from insulated boots to hip waders as we crisscrossed the tundra looking for goose nests. We spent a fair bit of time in one of two wooden observation towers that had been set up along the shore of the bay, about a mile and a half from camp. From that vantage point we could count geese and read the alphanumeric codes on the plastic neckbands that some of them wore.

One day in July I was in one of these observation towers with my friend and field partner Barry Allen. We had gone to the tower to make some repairs after a series of long, hard winters snapped most of its guy wires and caused the wooden tower to list slightly. We also planned to count adult geese and their broods on the coastal flats along the bay. Having decided to make our observations first and work on the tower later, we climbed up and set up the tripod and spotting scope.

While scanning for the large "gang broods" of geese (breeding pairs of geese will often join their broods together, forming large groups of juveniles that can number in the dozens), we spotted a whitish lump about half a mile or so to the north. We initially passed it off as just another one of those white rocks strewn along the coast that in bright sunlight can look like bears. Only this rock seemed to have fur . . . , and eventually it swung its huge head around to sniff at a shift in the breeze.

So this rock was a bear . . .

We kept an eye on him, swinging the spotting scope around between counts to make sure we knew where he was. It would be an interesting walk back to camp if we lost track of him. Calling out numbers while Barry recorded them on his clipboard, I made my next scan of the birds just south of the tower and then spun back around to check on our bear.

Gone. Wrong spot? No, gone. I shifted the scope first to the left and then to the right, scanning for the bear, but found nothing. On the third or fourth swing of the lens toward the water I saw him, up and walking, lifting his head to one side to test the breeze off the bay, and heading our way. I called out to Barry, who looked up from the clipboard and whipped his head around.

"Where?" was his only word.

"Along the water, coming this way," I whispered, as if the bear were close enough to hear.

"I got him," said Barry, training his binoculars north.

Maybe the bear caught our movement in the tower, maybe he picked up our scent on the breeze, or maybe it was just time to move south along the coast in search of carcasses. Whatever the reason, the bear was making right for us. We kept binoculars and scope focused on him as he made his way down the beach. His movements were mesmerizing—head raised high to the breeze while his front legs alternately swung out in wide arcs from his massive body, muscle and sinew mimicking the hydraulic action of some great machine. The grace and patience of his movements belied the fact that he could run as fast as a horse, was as agile as a gymnast, and could chase down any human who looked like lunch.

"Kind of wish we had fixed the tower first, eh?"

We looked out at the snapped guy wires, hanging limp in the light breeze, like boiled noodles. Polar bears are known to pound on crusted snow and ice with their front paws to break through to capture seals in their lairs. The bears will also smash their way into cabins—through doors or windows or the roof, if the snow is high enough. Until the camp managers learned that every bit of food or anything that might contain the scent of food had to be flown out of camp at the end of each field season, just about every year our first chore was repairing the damage to the wooden Quonset hut. We would joke about polar bears' not having a reverse gear, because they never seemed to go out the same way they came in—they'll break in through the roof, pilfer the joint, and bust out through a wall. Now we were wondering whether two biologists in a wooden tower would seem like a good meal, just waiting for this bear to come, pound on the pillars, and push the tower over.

The next few seconds were a scramble. I can't quite remember if we checked the shotgun or our cameras first, but everything was loaded and we crouched down breathlessly as we watched the bear approach. He was traveling on a straight line toward us now. There was no mistaking it—he was heading for the tower.

Even at the approach of so massive a carnivore I had no sense of danger or fear. I figured we were pretty safe in the tower, despite its condition. I was excited and filled with awe. This was a defining moment. I was on my first job as a biologist, twenty feet up in a tower on the coast of Hudson Bay, thirty miles from the town of Churchill, six hundred miles from the city of Winnipeg, and a long way from home.

The bear was getting closer—fifty feet out and still advancing. We were burning through film like crazy men. The clicks of the camera shutters now had the bear's full attention, and predators are nothing if not curious, so on he came.

The bear arrived at the tower and approached to within ten feet of the base. He was right below us. Then he did something that we did not quite expect—he paused. He just stopped and looked up, leaning slightly to one side, at about the same angle as the tower itself. His head bobbed as he sampled the air for information. I was still furiously clicking away, and then, abruptly, I paused too. All I could hear was the whir of Barry's autoadvance as the rest of the world fell silent.

My mouth open, I looked down into the face of the bear as he looked up at me. His head was pointed and seal-like, with tiny black eyes and small rounded ears. The fur was white but tinged with yellow, a bit dirty around the legs and belly. His paws were absolutely massive,

like snow shovels with claws. His nose was always working, tasting the wind for clues. And his face was simply serene; passive and handsome but betraying maybe a trace of puzzlement. There was no malice, no ferocity, no blood lust, just some calm sense of curiosity and a look that I can only recall as awareness, of us and everything around him.

He looked up at us from his world, and after a few minutes moved to his left, rounded the tower, and heading off through the light mist that shrouded the coastline to the south, continued on his way.

Twenty years later and some fifteen hundred miles to the southeast I watch another creature make its way across a very different kind of landscape. In central Massachusetts on an October morning I bring my vehicle up short because I've caught some movement out of the corner of my eye. A lone coyote is crossing a field. She is moving in the same direction as my vehicle but angling away from me, alternately turning her head to look my way and turning away again as she makes for a break in the fence line. She's not running but is moving along at a pretty good clip, as if she has somewhere to be. Just beyond the field lies a row of suburban houses, built sometime in the last ten years, where once there were more fields and unoccupied woodlots. Not too concerned about my presence, probably more curious than anything, because most cars she sees are moving and rarely stop, the coyote keeps a casual eye on me. In a couple of minutes she slips through the fence and passes along the border of the backyards, disappearing into the shrubby undergrowth, traveling as if she's been this way many times before.

The coyote is an American success story. The species has persevered in the face of hardship and persecution throughout its geographic range. In the West, government agents and ranchers waged war against the coyote, by poisoning, trapping, and shooting in an attempt to reduce its numbers. Despite the concerted effort, coyote populations never seemed to diminish, even during the twentieth century, when new techniques and new technology accounted for the deaths of millions of individuals. Folks in the East were disgusted with the slaughter and were unconcerned about the large losses that coyotes could cause to the livestock industry (over $40 million a year).[3] Now that we suspect that coyotes may kill and eat some of our pets, we in the East wage a war of our own against the species. It is nothing the coyote hasn't seen before, so it adjusts and moves in the suburban terrain just the way it has on the plains and prairies of the West. Coyotes go where the food is, and since they consume all manner of small and large mammals, birds, berries, insects, and fruits and scavenge as well as hunt, they can find something to eat anyplace in America—in the mountains, deserts, prairies, woods. It turns out that suburbs offer many resources: mice, squirrels, chipmunks, birds, garbage by the garage, dog food on the back porch, occasionally a pet cat out for an evening stroll.

The coyote is an American icon. It symbolizes freedom and independence and wildness. It reminds us of that renegade streak that we like to see in ourselves and in our national character. My guess is that the most intolerant rancher in the West likes having at least a few of these animals around, although he might not admit it to his neighbors. Coyotes have always represented the West in our country, but now they connect West and East, dissolving the false dichotomy and joining us—Easterner and Westerner—together. Coyotes will traverse the Rocky Mountains in summer and amble over the Mississippi River in winter. They'll lope across the prairies and move through the forest, skirting the edge of town in daylight and traveling through it after dark, always moving onward in search of new opportunities, just like us.

The coyote represents a return to nature, though not one of our choosing—we are way too caught up in a world of our own creation to make the transition back to nature ourselves. The coyote represents nature returning to us, uninvited and unexpected. We live in our comfortable suburban homes, connected to one another through cables and satellites. The wooded hills and watercourses are fragmented into housing developments and shopping centers. The world is dominated by humans and so very different from the way it was two hundred short years ago. But the coyote is here, waiting outside the kitchen door. It is not howling to its domestic dog cousins—it is calling to us. We may not like the sound, or everything the coyote represents, but it is back in all its toothy, furry glory. Sure, its presence in the driveway may make us nervous, we may have no idea what the coyote is up to, and we may wonder just how worried we should be. The question is, what do we do about it? In many places hunting and trapping as a way to control animal populations is now either unacceptable or impractical, so we may look up the number of the nearest pest control agent. If that doesn't work, we can call and complain to the state wildlife agency and tell the officials to come out and deal with "their" coyote. Nevertheless, the coyote somehow manages to get by, even if its presence in our neighborhood tries our patience and tests our tolerance of the natural world.

Nature is, after all, all around us, pulsing and breathing and spying on us, as if we were fish in a bowl. Despite all we do to coax it into neat rows and tended landscaping, in the places we live nature comes back, surviving in our world but on its own terms, and adapting to the changes we have demanded of it. Nature forces plantains up through the cracks in our driveway, distributes dandelions across our lawn, invites house sparrows into our eaves and skunks under our foundation. It opens up our garbage cans for raccoons and offers the produce of our gardens to rabbits. Nature is starlings in the birdbath and bats up under the siding. It sounds like crickets in the basement or squirrels running across the roof. It looks like the track of a deer in the flower bed. And sometimes it wears the face of a coyote.

CHAPTER 1

The World's Neighborhoods

🌿 In the foothills of the Andes Mountains in northern Peru, Mike and I stand on a rocky outcrop. We are sweating lightly and breathing heavily from the climb. Behind us are the tall peaks of the Andes; before us, the broad sweep of an unoccupied valley. We are in condor country, in the territory of a breeding pair of Andean condors, one of two species of condors in the world.

In the United States, the California condor—the other species of condor—is endangered. It earned that status by having its numbers drop to twenty-two in 1982. What is more, the condor has become a symbol of endangerment.[1] And although the term "endangered species" has lost some of its impact, owing to overuse, misunderstandings, and politics, the "endangered" in "endangered species" still means in danger of extinction. And the extinction of a species means that it and everything it represents in our world are gone forever. If California condors go extinct, there will never, ever be another species exactly like them—God or evolution through all the time in the universe will never make another.

During the mid-1980s so few California condors were left in the wild that biologists deemed it necessary to take the remaining birds into captivity for breeding. The hope was that one day wild condors could be coaxed to produce young in the relative safety of a zoo, and the fledglings could eventually be released into the wild.

Back in the early 1980s Mike Wallace and Stan Temple of the University of Wisconsin had been studying techniques of captive breeding and release for condors. Andean condors did not need the help but California condors did, and anything Mike and Stan could learn about condors in the remote regions of Peru could eventually be used to release California condors back into the wild in North America. This in fact came to pass: at the Grand Canyon in Arizona for example. After several years without any free-ranging condors, by the late 1990s North America had a few of these huge birds living wild over some of our most stunning landscapes.

But on that day in 1984 we had climbed to that ridge in northern Peru to see Andean condors—only this pair was nowhere in sight, so we stood for a while, taking in the scenery. We had followed a trail up along a waterless creek bed, steep in places, rocky throughout. We had driven miles off-road just to reach the base of these hills, through some of the most remote country I have ever seen. It was dry—the land and the air—and now my throat constricted a bit for want of water.

We could see where the pair had had their nest in some previous season, but they would not breed this year, and without young to feed, the adults were free to roam farther and longer. Given the broad expanse that makes up their foraging area and the distance they can cover on those huge wings, they could be anywhere.

It was getting on toward dusk and, figuring and hoping to see the birds the next day, we were thinking about making camp for the night. The valley below was just beginning to darken, showing no flickering lights, just shapes and shadows. I felt the absence of people now in the early evening as I had felt the heat during the middle of the day—as a force or feeling that is hard to explain. Then suddenly, without warning, the condors appeared, popping up over a distant ridge almost simultaneously, like two helium balloons tethered together. They must have ridden the thermals up the far side. Even at this distance they looked huge. They saw us as soon as we saw them, and with the slightest tilt of their wings, they cut an arc through the air and made directly for us.

The distance between us and them vanished in an instant, and before we could say anything at all, the pair was flying just feet in front of us. The male came first, and we thought we might reach out and touch him before he turned and looped around once more. The female followed, cruising by us almost as close. The male wore a fleshy crest, and both had powdery white feather collars. Their crops were distended, clear-cut evidence that they had found some of the carrion that sustains them.

They made numerous passes back and forth, so close that we could count feathers and see the light reflected in their eyes. We watched, speechless, until they turned and drifted off below the ridge.

Much of the world is looking less and less like that remote valley in northern Peru. Urban centers grow like amoebas in all developed, and most developing, nations, where they extend over the land, as more and more people move from rural areas to the cities to look for work, or leave urban centers for the city's edge, to look for a better place to live. In many nations in the world, a ring of suburban development encircles metropolitan areas—we may not mind working in the city, but many of us would rather not, or cannot afford to, live there, and thus bedroom communities spring up along the outskirts of the city and spread outward into the rural landscape. Our ability and willingness to commute from home to work—whether physically or electronically—only encourages this trend.

Urbanization is the name given to the process whereby the landscape is developed through human settlement and occupation. Roads, water and sewer lines, and power grids are laid out. Factories, apartments, schools, and malls are erected. Parking lots appear. In conjunction with the new construction, the local vegetation and sometimes even the topography are scraped away or transformed. Woodlots are drastically thinned, if not entirely cleared away. Hills are leveled, low spots graded, wetlands filled. In the desert the most charismatic of the cacti, such as giant saguaros and ocotillos, are uprooted and transplanted—these can be worth a lot of money to landscapers and real estate agents. The rest of the land is bladed and scraped to make way for new developments. In grasslands and on old farms or agricultural land the process of urbanization may be easiest of all. The building sites are usually already cleared of most of the denser vegetation and are relatively flat. A bit of fill and a few hours of heavy-equipment operation can be all that is needed to prepare a site. Let the building begin.

Another word for this process of transforming the landscape is "sprawl." In this sense, "sprawl" was actually coined back in 1937 by Earle Draper, who has been called one of the first city planners in the United States. Some people object to the use of the term to refer to the growth of cities because of the negative connotations, but "sprawl" does conjure up an image of the haste and lack of long-range planning that often do go into the spread of urban and suburban areas. It is the scale and extent of the development and the mind-boggling rate of change that really give "sprawl" its meaning and have made the word a permanent part of our modern lexicon. Are any of us not dumbfounded by the rate at which the transformation of the American landscape is taking place? Certainly it would be hard to find metropolitan centers that are not growing like well-fed amoebas. To witness the pace of change, if you are not observing it firsthand in the place where you live now, return to a town or city where you grew up or lived for a time five or ten years ago, and see whether it hasn't changed almost past recognition. Growth of this kind has been happening for quite some time and is likely to continue well into the future. It's just that now it seems to be happening everywhere, and faster.[2]

Traditionally, the term "urban areas" is used to refer to cities, like Boston, Chicago, Los Angeles, Seattle, London, Sydney, or Tokyo. These are places dominated by concrete and steel, tall buildings, heavily used roads, and high human population density. Historically, suburbs or something like them first came into being in the 1800s in the eastern United States, where people could travel by rail from outlying areas to nearby big cities. The suburbs we are familiar with today are a more recent phenomenon, made possible in the mid-twentieth century by the availability of affordable and convenient transportation—namely, automobiles—that could transport people from home to work and back. Suburbs today are dominated by stand-alone single-family homes, fenced yards, strip malls, and the occasional swimming pool. In general, human population density is lower in the suburbs than in the city, but much higher than in rural communities.

Some writers have recommended defining and standardizing the terms we use to describe varying levels of development—for example, the percentage of human-made structures, sometimes called the built environment (buildings, bridges, roads), that covers the land, the density of buildings, and human density could be used to define and distinguish urban from suburban and rural from exurban areas. In an urban area, for instance, more than 50 percent of the land might be developed—having, say, more than four buildings and four residents per acre, or ten buildings and ten residents per hectare (since scientists often prefer to work with round numbers, and with the metric system). A suburban area would be defined as 30 to 50 percent built environment, with about two to ten buildings and more than ten residents per hectare. Rural areas would have lower densities of buildings and people, and wildlands would show very little if any development (say,

0 to 2 percent) and few if any residents (less than one person per hectare).[3] True wilderness would harbor no buildings and no human residents and would, in the purest sense, be unmarred by any recent human activity.

All this quantification of the landscape is useful, especially in light of computers and geographic information systems (GIS), but perhaps a bit difficult to visualize. On a working basis I think of urban areas as lands with high population density, tall buildings, well-developed infrastructure, prominent industry and business, and lots of noise. Suburban areas are characterized by moderate to high population density and are zoned for mostly residential development, particularly detached single-family homes, with supporting infrastructure, retail businesses, and some noise. Rural areas have low population density and agricultural lands, woodlots, and natural areas, interspersed with some residences. What noise there is in rural areas generally comprises the different kinds of sounds that are often heard early in the morning: machinery starting up, roosters crowing, chainsaws in the spring, or gunshots during the hunting season in the fall. Such noises don't bother me much. I like the sounds and smells of the country and I am usually up early anyway, but they do often disturb the modified tranquility of outlying suburban developments, whose homes frequently border farms and whose transplanted residents are now neighbors with the rural folk. A common refrain in urbanizing America is that rural settings are nice to look at; but just don't be starting up your tractor at 5 A.M. . . . and can't there be something done about that smell?

Wildlands are all we have left that we haven't built on, but we may graze cattle, cut down trees, mine in it, recreate on it, or otherwise mark our presence. This land can be classified as primarily nonagricultural, as well as by definition nonurban or exurban. Recreation and wildlife areas comprise 95 million acres, or 5 percent of all land in the continental United States. The total jumps to about 750 million acres or 40 percent of the U.S. land base, excluding Alaska, if you count forest lands and "areas of little surface use," such as marshes, open swamps, bare rock, desert, and tundra. If pasture and range are included, we can add another 578 million acres and raise the percentage to 70 percent of the lower forty-eight states. Cows graze on most of this open and undeveloped country, a consideration that will bother those people known as conservation biologists but not others, known as ranchers. At any rate, impressively large tracts of our country are not part of the built environment. The remainder is mostly croplands (about 350 million acres or 18 percent of the continental United States) and land for "other uses," including cities and towns. Urban land comprises over 70 million acres in the United States and has been increasing by an average of about one and a half million acres a year since 1990.[4]

At the far end of the spectrum is wilderness, "where the hand of man has never set foot," as they say. We won't really consider wilderness in this book, except to touch briefly on two points. First, wilderness has represented a fulcrum in our relation to the land since the beginning of our nation. Wilderness was at first feared, challenged, and then tamed; later, as it became rare, it became something to be championed, protected, and cherished, at least by some. The balance tipped toward the latter with the passage of the Wilderness Act in 1964. Formulated by Howard Zahniser of the Wilderness Society and signed into law by President Lyndon B. Johnson on September 3, 1964, the Wilderness Act created the National Wilderness Preservation System. It is clear that the author and Congress had in mind the effects of continued growth and development, for section 2(a) begins: "In order to assure that an increasing population, accompanied by expanding settlement and growing mechanization, does not occupy and modify all areas within the United States and its possessions, leaving no lands designated for preservation and protection in their natural condition, it is hereby declared to be the policy of the Congress to secure for the American people of present and future generations the benefits of an enduring resource of wilderness."[5]

The act provides this definition of wilderness: "A wilderness, in contrast with those areas where man and his own works dominate the landscape, is hereby recognized as an area where the earth and its community of life are untrammeled by man, where man himself is a visitor who does not remain." The act also refers to wilderness as land that retains its primeval character and influence, without permanent improvements or human habitation, and generally appears to have been affected primarily by the forces of nature; the imprint of human presence is not substantially noticeable. The act recognizes that wilderness offers outstanding opportunities for solitude or a "primitive and unconfined" type of recreation and that such expanses may also contain ecological, geological, or other features of scientific, educational, scenic, or historical value. The idea of wilderness is one of America's most inspired revelations. It is what the writer Wallace Stegner, a supporter of the Wilderness Act, described as "the geography of hope."[6]

This all sounds pretty different from what we know as the suburbs. In fact, wilderness really is an entity altogether different from those mentioned previously—cities and suburbia. These days "wilderness" may almost represent more of a philosophy or a concept than serve as a word that truly defines an area or describes a landscape. The saddest thing may be that it could be maintained that no true wilderness at all is left on earth: even the remotest places on the planet feel the weight of human presence in some way. Winds carry dust, smoke, and sulfates from one side of the world to the other; global warming is changing vegetation patterns in Alaska and melting the sea ice in the high arctic; and a gap exists in the ozone layer in the sky above the continent of Antarctica.[7] Even that remote valley in northern Peru where we saw the condors showed signs of human use: two-track trails and roads, grazing of livestock, cutting of firewood. Perhaps the deepest trenches in the deepest parts of the oceans may remain untouched by human activity, but who knows what we will find as we start to explore those places further. The truth is, we humans and our works and activities have marked every place on earth. In both prehistoric and modern times we have crossed oceans, traversed mountain ranges, hopscotched from island to island, and spread out over continents, directing the course of nature as we go. And now we have taken the first tiny steps into space . . . always moving onward in search of new opportunities.[8]

We tend to view suburbs as separate from the city, especially as new developments become more self-contained, with their own shopping centers, golf courses, and schools. I grew up thinking this way. I was born and raised in a suburb of Boston but didn't know much more about the city than someone from northern New Hampshire would, and I never thought of myself as a Bostonian. Back then, Watertown was a separate place; almost a stand-alone town. But like all things in nature, the suburbs are in some way connected to everything else: they are not separate from the city, or from rural areas or even wild places, for that matter. In many regions of this country and the world as a whole, urban development follows a gradient as it moves from the dense core at the heart of the business district of a city to the surrounding suburban neighborhoods to the farm fields or woodlots or patches of desert on the edge of town to the residual wild or natural world. Of course, landscape patterns and processes are often more complicated than this representation: communities spring up and grow at various points along the way, thus creating smaller gradients within the larger ones. Yet the urban-to-rural or urban-to-natural progression is real.[9]

Massachusetts is one good example: drive along Route 2 or the Mass Turnpike from Boston to the Berkshire Mountains, and you will see what I mean. A general urban-to-rural gradient runs from east to west, as do lesser gradients that flow out of smaller (but growing) urban centers such as Worcester, Springfield, and Pittsfield. Just remember, when you are out in the Berkshires on a nice fall day, what happens in the city and suburbs of Boston to the east affects the hills and valleys in the west—politically, socially, economically, and ecologically. Sprawl moves in many ways.

It takes land, resources, and people to create sprawl, and the United States is wealthy in all three. This country is particularly rich in land. The first of many apparent dichotomies is that despite the rapid spread of urban, suburban, commercial, and recreational development and the concern that it causes, the overall land base is only about 2–3 percent developed; the land remains 97 to 98 percent rural (and partially agricultural) or undeveloped.[10] This varies from state to state, of course. In the large states of the Rocky Mountain region, northern Great Plains, and desert Southwest less than 1 percent of the land is developed. Many midwestern and southeastern states have a large proportion of agricultural land, but only 2 to 5 percent of land is given over to urban or suburban development. It is not until we come to the northeastern United States that we find more than 5 percent of the land base under development—except of course in Florida, where many people from the Northeast move to escape the hard winters. Four states in the Northeast, with a little over 20 percent of their land base under development, lead the pack on sprawl: New Jersey, Connecticut, Rhode Island, and Massachusetts.

The figures on the vast expanses of U.S. land not under development lead some people to challenge the idea that sprawl is bad, or that it is even happening. They ask, If only 2 percent of the nation's entire land base is developed, where is the problem?[11] In a sense they are right. Even in a state like Massachusetts, 80 percent or so of the landscape is still devoted to farms, small communities, low-density residential development, state forests, wildlife management areas, and other undeveloped or relatively undeveloped uses. And Massachusetts is small: at about 8,200 square miles, it is the sixth-smallest state, behind Rhode Island, Delaware, Connecticut, Hawaii, and New Jersey. If we combined all six New England states, we would have a landmass the size of a respectable western state, like Washington or North Dakota, say. Then the figure for developed land would stand at about 6 percent, a percentage more in line with the national norm.

Part of the problem, however, as ecologists and other citizens who are concerned about urban sprawl see it, is not so much overall national land use patterns, but the toll that sprawl takes on the natural resource base. Sprawl is closely linked with resource consumption: more and bigger homes, higher energy demands, embarrassingly extravagant water consumption. We have more energy-efficient dwellings and appliances, but the increase in both people and gadgets translates into a need for more power to heat, to cool, and to operate. According to the National Association of Home Builders, the average American home has more than doubled in size over the past half a century or so, from 983 square feet in 1950 to 2,350 square feet in 2002.[12] All this resource consumption has led some researchers to estimate the size of the ecological "footprint" of a city, a town, or even a single home—that is, how many resources and of which kind—energy, water, space—does it take to maintain that city or town or single-family dwelling? In the final analysis, our footprint on the globe is huge and getting larger, and population size and affluence are the "principal drivers" of this phenomenon.[13]

We have a long reach. Think about the desert cities of Las Vegas, Phoenix, and Tucson. How is their voracious appetite for water fed? Much of it comes from underground aquifers, and those cities are mining (in other words, using up) that water at a great rate, so much so that the average depth of a well dug in the Tucson basin has increased significantly. People had to drill down fifty feet or so to reach water in the early 1900s, but must often go several times deeper today, as a result of drops in the water table of more than two hundred feet in some places. We also drain water from the Colorado River to such an extent that the flow of freshwater from the river no longer reaches its delta in Mexico. A wetland ecosystem that Aldo Leopold once referred to as "a common home in the remote fastness of space and time," for both people and wildlife, no longer exists.[14] And now it is likely that we will soon be piping water to the Southwest from as far away as the Pacific Northwest or Canada. All this water goes toward growing crops in the dry lands of the Southwest or into the swimming pools, reflecting ponds, water fountains, lawns, golf courses, and flush toilets of our shining desert cities.

And of course we drive. Collectively, Americans consume some 10–20 million barrels of oil or 300–400 million gallons of gas per day—well over 100 billion gallons per year. All this gas consumption causes drilling rigs to spring up in places as far away as the tundra of northern Alaska and the remote valleys of the Rocky Mountains, and of course in many, many other places throughout the world. We want that oil so that we can commute great distances to work. We put up with the traffic because (1) we can live in a nicer place if we commute, (2) we can live in a more affordable place if we commute, and (3) public transportation is a drag. About 90 percent of us drive to work in our personal vehicle, many of us alone, because it is more convenient and we can come and go when we want to.[15] When we are not dodging potholes and traffic, we telecommute to work on our personal computers in our home offices, checking e-mail, sending reports as attachments, and navigating the Internet the same way we pick alternate travel routes to the office. All this allows us to live farther from the cities and towns where we work and to move out into the suburbs or countryside.

Of all the numbers we can cite regarding land use patterns and resource consumption, the most compelling is our own headcount. Urbanization is fueled by the most staggering figure of all—that of the burgeoning human population. More than six billion people live on earth now, an incomprehensible number that no longer means much to most of us, so far does it lie beyond our comprehension. Worldwide, the greatest numbers of people live in Asia, Africa, and Latin America. Those of us living in North America can thus largely ignore the situation, given our comparatively low population density and abundant wealth and resources. The population of the United States continues to grow, however, and much of our future population growth will be fueled not by births, but by immigration.[16] In 2009 the Population Reference Bureau reported that on the basis of population size the United States ranks third in the world (at 307 million), behind China (1.3 billion) and India (1.1 billion). In the year 2050 the bureau estimates that the United States will still be third (at 439 million), behind India (1.7 billion) and China (1.4 billion), and that the total world population will exceed nine billion. Many of us living today will still be alive then.

For the past two centuries the world's population has become increasingly urban, but especially during the twentieth century. In the United States less than 5 percent of the population was considered urban in 1790; today more than 80 percent of U.S. citizens live in cities and towns, and less than 20 percent or so in rural communities. The same holds true for the rest of the world: only about 2 percent of people lived in cities in 1800; today more than 50 percent of the world's population lives in cities, and the number is growing. With increasing urbanization cities are reaching extraordinary sizes. In 1900 there were no cities with ten million people. New York City (actually the city proper and its metropolitan area) passed that mark in 1950. By 2000, nineteen cities throughout the world had ten million people or more, but only four of these—Tokyo, Osaka, New York, and Los Angeles—

were in industrialized nations.[17] As cities get bigger, they expand outward, claiming space and resources like a living thing and leaving more and bigger "footprints" on the surface of the earth.

Urbanization represents a building and a tearing down, progress in one sense but great losses in another. The most obvious of these is the loss of open space, and with it a sense of tranquility and a connection to nature. It is another example of the dichotomies that define us as a species and as a driving force on our planet. We build magnificent cities, modern medical facilities, great seats of government and institutions of higher education, innovative art museums, concert halls, and sports arenas, elaborate, safe, and secure housing—truly wonderful places to live—and yet our consumption—squandering—of vast quantities of resources threatens many life-forms, including our own. I am not saying that we shouldn't live well or that we all don't have a right to a good home and adequate resources; but we need to ask ourselves— all of us, collectively, as human beings, without pointing a finger at a subset of people such as loggers, ranchers, builders, or commercial fishermen—Is it truly necessary to use all the resources on earth to the point of exhaustion? Fresh water, clean air, topsoil, marine fish, old-growth timber . . . we use them all up at great rates and then, when we are faced with impending shortages and an uncertain future, practice denial and blame. What about open space? We view it as just another commodity, one that has always seemed to be in endless supply.

You have probably seen the NASA image from space of the earth at night.[18] The now-famous photograph is actually a composite of satellite images that shows the concentration of artificial lights all over the world. Some pockets of darkness still remain, in the Amazon basin, central Africa, central Australia, and even some parts of the United States (Wyoming and Alaska), but by and large the trail of lights marks our universal passage into urbanization. The lights are particularly prevalent in parts of the United States, Europe, and Asia, especially along the coasts. I don't even want to say too much about it, except to urge you to go to the Internet, find a copy of this picture, and just look at it again. What you will see is a pattern of human dispersal and settlement and progress on the earth. Our way is lit by our own artificial lights, and they shine like the eyes of humanity—all six billion of us—looking up from our home into space.

In a grassy field in Massachusetts, in the shadows formed by the late afternoon sun shining through a small grove of trees, a solitary coyote lies, head up, surveying the field in front of her. The light, which blends with the grizzled grays and tawny browns and yellows of her coat as she straddles the shadow line, camouflages her and blurs the edges of her form until they merge with the landscape. Forty yards away, cars whiz by at speeds twenty to thirty miles over the posted limit and houses dot the edge of the meadow before the density of homes increases just beyond the woodlot. Her ears rotate slightly toward the sounds of kids shouting and playing in nearby backyards and a dog barking some distance away, but nobody sees the coyote as she lies listening for rustling in the grass and watching for movement among the trees on the opposite side of the meadow. Come evening, she will make her rounds of the garbage cans alongside garages and the pet food dishes left by backdoors. She will leave droppings on the edge of the lawn that will go unnoticed and wet tracks in the driveway that will fade as the sun comes up, and she'll be back in this meadow for a morning nap before anyone is the wiser.

The coyote is one creature that has learned to make the most of suburban circumstances. It is not alone in its ability to exploit human environments, but the coyote has certainly captured our attention. There is nothing like a threat to human safety—whether real or merely perceived—to grab headlines and ratchet up public anxiety. Coyotes are small carnivores by comparison with mountain lions or the timber wolves, but when compared with the animals we are used to seeing in our neighborhoods, they are huge. Actually, coyotes are about as big as a medium-sized dog, not quite so robust or heavy as a German shepherd. When a coyote's fur is wetted down, or in the hellishly hot, dry conditions of the Southwestern desert, where the coat of the animal is thin and its body scrawny, it can look pretty small. But I have also seen coyotes in eastern Oregon, well fed on jackrabbits, mice, and carrion, furred out for the cold of winter, that looked so large that you might mistake them for wolves. The eastern coyote is actually one of the biggest subspecies of coyote, with adults measuring up to fifty-something inches in body length, plus some fifteen inches or so of tail. Males,

which are larger than females, weigh in at thirty-five to forty pounds (fifty to sixty pounds is possible but rare). Females are usually five to ten pounds lighter than males. Many breeds of domestic dogs outweigh coyotes.

Coyotes are relative newcomers to the Northeast. They were originally a canid of the prairies and grasslands of the American West, creatures of far horizons and open spaces. But they are also travelers, and given a chance they will wander beyond the boundaries of pre-Columbian ecology to establish themselves in all kinds of places. Apparently coyotes followed the trail of miners, and of their trash and dead horses and mules, up the Klondike Trail and into Alaska. In the past century or so they have moved in waves from their prairie home, west into California and south into Mexico. They have infiltrated the north woodlands, trading their former broad prairie vistas for heavily wooded haunts. And they have invaded the eastern United States, so thoroughly that when they got to the coast they crossed over sea ice or swam through the ocean to many of the islands off the Atlantic shore. The Elizabeth Islands off of Falmouth and Wood's Hole have coyotes; the islands of Martha's Vineyard and Nantucket do not. It may be unlikely that Vineyard Sound would freeze over enough to allow easy passage from the mainland to Martha's Vineyard, but if it were ever possible, coyotes could probably do it.

The movement of coyotes from their Western prairie home into most of the rest of the continental United States and southern Canada has been called a historic journey by the biologist and writer Gerry Parker. Parker describes the movement of coyotes into the eastern United States and Canada as a "story of unparalleled range expansion," because of the relative speed and completeness of the immigration. It is thought that human extirpation of the wolf in the East opened up the way for coyotes. Writing about our own movements on the continent in *Across the Wide Missouri,* the historian Bernard DeVoto states that "American history . . . is history in transition from an Atlantic to a Pacific phase."[19] Coyotes, whose ways so often run counter to the ways of humans, have reversed this migration; they have colonized the country in all directions, but the most astounding progression has been their movement from west to east.

Apparently, coyotes and I entered the scene in Massachusetts at about the same time. The first records of coyotes in the state date to the 1950s.[20] I claim neither kinship nor responsibility on that account; it is just one of those coincidental facts that I find interesting, and it makes me form a connection of sorts with them in my mind. Quite apart from that, I like coyotes for what they are, in spite of the strong feelings they elicit from citizens who hate what they do or might do, and from nature lovers who would coddle them and represent them as something they are not. Coyotes do not play by our rules—never have, never will. Yet they have moved into our suburbs and have adapted to the changes better than I have myself. Perhaps that is one reason they fascinate me and make me want to watch what they do.

CHAPTER 2

The Form Setter

🐾 Round Island lies eleven miles off the coast of Alaska, in Bristol Bay. The small island is nestled in a crook in the coastline formed by Cape Pierce to the north and the Aleutian Archipelago to the south, where the island chain begins its long, sweeping curve from the mainland out into the sea. At just over one square mile in size there is not much that stands out about this island in comparison to the vast Pacific to the west or the high mountains beyond the Nushagak Peninsula to the east, except on paper and during the summer. On paper, it is one of seven islands designated as the Walrus Island State Game Sanctuary by the Alaska Department of Fish and Game. During summer, it constitutes a haul-out and resting ground for some five thousand to fifteen thousand male Pacific walrus.

Round Island is a bit of a mystery. Its cliff faces are covered with more than 70,000 black-legged kittiwakes, 150,000 common murres, and uncounted cormorants, puffins, and guillemots during the nesting season, a profusion of birds that is certainly not unusual for rocky cliffs on the coast of Alaska. A small population of red foxes inhabiting the island gets by on a diet of tundra voles, birds, eggs, insects, and berries. The ability of the foxes to survive the winters on the island is impressive but foxes on islands are not such a strange phenomenon.[1] The absence of any large mammals such as caribou or bears on the island is a source of delight to botanists and lichenologists, and possibly to the plants and lichens themselves, but freedom from heavy grazing and trampling is more of a happy circumstance than a puzzle to ecologists.

But who knows why only relatively few walrus, and all of them males, make the journey each summer, in some cases hundreds of miles from the Chukchi Sea, to bask on the rocks of Round Island. Who knows when this summer tradition started, or how word got around within a cohort of bulls but not among their mothers and sisters. Many of the females, instead of coming south, go north in the summer, following the edge of the retreating sea ice to give birth and raise their young in the northern oceans.

These summer mysteries of southward migration and sexual segregation notwithstanding, the biggest puzzle is the life of the walrus itself. The walrus is an amazing animal. The scientist Francis Fay described it as "one of the most remarkable creatures in the Arctic."[2] Walrus, like most living things, are incredibly well adapted to a certain set of circumstances and conditions. For walrus, those conditions are dictated by arctic waters and ice, for they live most of their lives in or on the ocean. Males can grow to 3,750 pounds, much of the weight in blubber. That blubber, up to six inches thick, depending on the individual, the season, and the part of the body, protects them from frigid ocean temperatures and bitter arctic air. Only seasonally do they make their way to shore to bask in the sun. They arrive white as unbaked dough because freezing water temperatures force their blood to the core of their bodies, but leave a well-done reddish brown, once the sun has warmed them and brought blood back to the surface of their skin.[3]

It is along the thin margins of land and sea in a few places like Round Island that people and walrus meet, neither able to comprehend what the other's world is really like. We study walrus and understand a good deal about their habits, we visit their realm as we can, but we will never really know it as it is, lying still and frozen beneath the winter borealis and a brightness of stars, the memory of which has all but faded from the minds of humankind.

From a low ridge on the edge of the island I watch as walrus take the sun and then, in ones and twos, lumber over the rocks to reach the water, where they are transformed from undulating blubber into graceful swimmers, expelling blasts of breath and sucking in great lungfuls of air, before slipping beneath the surface and disappearing into the sea.

I grew up on the shores of a great city, amid a sea of suburban houses. Boston was six miles away—both very close and very far away. At the age of ten I could wade through traffic to the middle of our busy street and look east down the centerline to the Prudential Tower—the Pru, in the middle of Boston, the Hub, the center of the business district—rising above the concrete horizon like a blue sail on the distant Atlantic. I could then finish crossing the street, crawl under a fence, and be in the pine and oak woodlot just across from our house.

Watertown was both small town and big city, home to blue-collared townies who worked the graveyard shift at the B. F. Goodrich rubber plant and tweed-clad intellectuals who taught at Harvard and MIT. The town was a gridlike pattern of tightly bunched, mostly two- or three-family houses that merged into neighboring towns, its boundaries meaningless except to mapmakers, tax assessors, and the locals who had lived there all their lives. The sounds and smells of Italy and Ireland and Armenia invaded the colonial architecture and Yankee attitudes. Watertown was jammed with traffic and overrun with kids. It was, in every sense, a modern suburb in the New World.

Watertown in the 1950s and 1960s may not have been a place where anyone would knowingly have chosen to come into the world. Like all hometowns, you were just born into it. By the middle of the last century, time and traffic and concrete and congestion had filled it up and worn it down. Some of the colonial charm was no doubt still there, but much of it was covered over with weathered asphalt, dulled vinyl, and many layers of old paint.[4]

An age ago the region was home to Pequossette and Nonantum, and these people lived along the rivers or at the coast, where they fished, farmed, gathered, and hunted. They built wooden longhouses near the shore in summer and hide-covered wigwams farther inland during the winter. The Pequossette and Nonantum were subsidiary tribes of the Massachuset Indians, who were closely related to the Wampanoag and Narragansett. Tribal relationships were varied and complex, and in those days, long before modern Americans developed the land and built their own cities and suburbs, southern New England was heavily populated. Today there are no longer any people known as the Massachuset. Most were wiped out by disease, war, slavery, and missionary zeal soon after the arrival of Europeans.[5]

In May 1630 Roger Clapp and his party made landing on a steep bank along the Charles River, not far from where my parents' house stands now. They met some of the Pequossette people, and Indians and Englishmen traded a bass for a biscuit. Clapp and his party moved on to settle in what is now Dorchester. Later, in July, a small group of English men and women, some of whom arrived on the *Arabella*, made a landing a little farther downriver. This group was led by Sir Richard Saltonstall and his minister George Phillips, and they called the place Saltonstall's Plantation.[6]

Two months later, in September 1630, the name was changed to Watertown, and it became one of the original six towns of Massachusetts and one of the largest settlements on the continent. At one time it included all or parts of the modern towns of Weston, Waltham, Lincoln, Belmont, and Cambridge. Thanks to the combination of navigable waters and fertile land, the region quickly became an important center of manufacturing, trade, and business. In 1638 one Thomas Mayhew built the first gristmill in America, in what was to become Watertown Square, and the site blossomed into a thriving mill town. The metamorphosis continued, transforming it from a Puritan settlement to a hub of trade and commerce, and helped open the way westward to further exploration and development. Thus began the evolution of the Boston metropolitan area, almost four hundred years ago, into a great city with sprawling suburbs.

In the late 1700s Watertown was the provincial capital of Massachusetts and a site of Revolutionary enterprise. George Washington and Paul Revere were active in the area, and relations among citizens continued to be "marked by frequent disputes, a penchant for questioning authority, and an atmosphere of tension and discord," as noted in the town's early history.[7]

By the early 1800s, wealthy Bostonians had bought up much of the Watertown area, where they could build country estates and escape the city from time to time, especially during the heat of the summer.[8] The nineteenth century also transformed the town and the region into a manufacturing mecca. People in factories large and small were busy making paper, dyes, clothing, sailcloth (some of it woven for the USS *Constitution*), chocolate, and later, rubber tires for bicycles, dry plates for cameras, and Crawford stoves. From 1816 to 1829, one of the first arsenals in America, the Watertown Arsenal, was built near the banks of the Charles. The arsenal originally served for ammunition storage, but in the next century the complex of buildings would play a role in research on arms and matériel for World War II, before being transformed, like so many of our historical landmarks, and like our open space, into a mall, a parking lot, a housing development, a small park. In the 1890s electric trolley cars were introduced, and in 1897 the first Stanley Steamer rolled out onto the unpaved streets. Gridlock was only a few decades away. Wealthier residents could relieve tension (or perhaps add to it) at one of the country's first golf courses, the Oakley Country Club, which was built in 1898.[9] Today it is one of the biggest patches of "open space," of a sort, in the area.

Over time the town shrank in area but grew in population. Today, about 33,000 people live in 4.2 square miles. By the 1950s, Watertown was already crowded and overbuilt, overwhelmed by traffic and lacking in open space. Any open space that was available was soon parceled out for more building lots. Even homes with large yards were subdivided, so that other houses could be jammed in between the existing buildings. Greenbacks, not green spaces, were the measure of progress, and open space was a concept barely recognized and not much talked about.

One saving grace has always been the Charles River.[10] John Smith had at first given it the name the Massachusetts in the early 1600s, but it was later changed in honor of King Charles I. The Charles winds past Watertown Square and down along the southern edge of town, making its slow way toward Boston Harbor. It is the water that gave the town its name and its life, but when I was growing up, the Charles was polluted. My grandfather used to swim in it back when he was a kid, but we would never have dreamed of doing so in the 1960s. I would sometimes wade up to my ankles along the shallow edges in search of frogs along the bank; everyone was sure I would come down with some nasty disease. Usually we just crossed over on rocks and tried to get nothing wet but the bottoms of our sneakers, as we peered into the black water and the vegetation along the shore.

Whatever Watertown lacked in open space, the local kids made up for in sheer ingenuity, with their inherent ability always to find places to play and explore. The town Web site lists as open space "parks, cemeteries, and riverbanks," a description that does give the right idea: they were small parcels or strips of land scattered among and surrounded by neighborhoods and businesses. Our parents and grandparents passed down no fields or swimming holes to us as places to play, so we would sneak down to the railroad tracks that bisected the town and hop the freighters for a slow ride into Brighton, or slip under the fence around the Perkins School for the Blind (famous for one of its former students, Helen Keller), and play on its grounds. We hung out in the backyards of friends and at a few of the town parks. We gathered at Saltonstall Park and the playground behind Phillips School, unaware of the history under our feet. Mostly we explored along the Charles River, on lands once administered by the Metropoli-

tan District Commission (or MDC, now the Department of Conservation and Recreation). The MDC maintained a strip of parkland running along the river through most of Watertown, and it was along the
banks and in the shallow water at the edge of this polluted river that I
undertook my first investigations of nature. My friend Dennis and I
would go down to the river every spring, as soon as we saw the lilacs in
bloom, to catch turtles and frogs, which we brought home and kept in
homemade terrariums or aquariums in the backyard or basement. The
river was where we first collected insects in jars and started birdwatching, with a shared pair of cheap binoculars and a brand-new
copy of Peterson's *A Field Guide to the Birds.*

Something about this town, with its cramped duplexed and triple-
decked neighborhoods and crowded gray streets, may have been a bit

tacky and mundane. I might have wished to be born instead in Maine or Montana or California. But Watertown had its good sides. It had its river, and back in the 1950s and '60s, it was filled with gardens. Not the manicured flower gardens of the wealthy, but the overflowing vegetable gardens of the lower and middle classes. People grew all kinds of things: zucchini, squash, beans, corn, potatoes, but especially tomatoes. The tomato was king. As far as we knew, the tomato was our town mascot, our state flower, our national emblem, and it was only for lack of foresight on the part of our founding fathers that it does not appear on the great seal of the town of Watertown.

I remember walking the back streets early on summer Sunday mornings, returning home after Mass at Saint Patrick's Church, and passing by those gardens, neatly tended and carefully protected by chain-link fences. Every square foot of dirt had something growing in it, fence line to fence line and up against the house. Some elderly man or woman always seemed to be in close attendance, leaning over to pull a weed, supported by one hand on a hoe. Usually the gardeners were so absorbed in what they were doing that they never noticed me; but sometimes they would turn at the right moment, smile, and without a word motion me over. Then, with a lightly spoken "For your mother," they would pass an armload of tomatoes over the fence. At this time of year no one really needed more tomatoes, but it was an act of kindness to offer them, and it would have been impolite to refuse. So I would bring them home and lay them on the kitchen table, with tiny clods of dirt still clinging to their sides, and my parents would say Wasn't that nice and wash them off in the sink.

My parents have lived their entire lives in this same town. My mom was born in Cambridge but moved soon afterward and was raised on Bacon Street in Watertown, just up the hill from the river. She worked right next door, in a small brick factory that once housed the Industrial String Company. That's where she met my dad, who also worked there. Both remember the jaw-rattling noise that went on every day in that little factory and claim that the tinnitus that they suffer today originated with their first jobs. My mom's dad—my grandfather—worked at Haartz-Mason Industries, a company that made rubberized fabrics and products. The building is still there on the banks of the

Charles. He was a dapper fellow, and I can picture him walking to work in his fedora hat and silk and wool vest, smoking a cigar, on a fine spring day in mid-twentieth-century Watertown.

My dad was from the West Side, and he remembers it when it was all farm fields and small orchards. There were twelve in his family living in a little eight-room house on Warren Street. When they moved up to North Beacon Street, where I was raised and where my parents still live, the road (now State Route 20) was literally a cow path that led to an abattoir in Brighton. My grandfather raised pigs and chickens in the backyard, which was one of those fence line–to–fence line gardens, and it seems that forever we had a grape arbor big enough to shelter a long picnic table and a lot of chairs underneath. Many families had arbors like that in those days, and people would gather under them for an early supper on a warm summer afternoon—an abundance of food spread out among grape leaf–shaped shadows on the worn boards.

My parents worked hard, lived pretty simply, and gave us everything they could. Few families were wealthy, but most of us had it all—loving families, secure homes, dozens of friends. Everyone's parents looked after everyone's kids, and discipline came not only from our parents but also from the mothers and fathers of friends, to the gratitude of our own parents, who promised to return the favor. We had no computers, no video games, no organized soccer leagues, although there was Little League baseball and Pop Warner football—some of us joined; most didn't. We watched television—simple shows uncomplicated by social consciousness or sexual innuendo—but mostly we played outside.

Of all the gifts our parents gave us, the most precious was time. Summers especially were endless, and we played hard and slept well. We would somehow all come together on a summer morning to play baseball—so many of us that we had two or three games going on at the same time. And again during a summer evening after supper, when waves of kids moved through the neighborhood playing capture the flag, while parents watched from front porches. Technology was no doubt prevalent and growing, as we moved from black-and-white to color, from standard to automatic, and eventually from pencils and pads of paper to keyboards and screens, but all these changes seemed less domineering and overwhelming and more intriguing and awe-inspiring back then, like a man walking on the moon.[11]

My birth certificate lists my father's occupation as "form setter." A form setter is the construction worker who builds the wooden forms to hold the concrete that becomes the foundation for a building. When I was born, my dad was building foundations for suburban homes in Watertown and the neighboring communities: setting and filling the forms, then stripping them for yet another house. At times, he tells me, they would build the foundation and move on to another job, in that way completing as many as ten foundations a week. At other times they would do it all—from the excavation and the footing to the roofing and the landscaping. It was demanding work out there in the elements. The heat in the summer was almost unbearable, as they worked down in the hole with the full sun reflecting off the oiled forms. The cold in winter was worse, when iron rebar could claim the skin from unprotected hands.

My father's dad before him had done the same thing, except that in my grandfather's day foundations were mostly dug by hand with picks and shovels. I cannot imagine how hard that work must have been anywhere, but especially here in New England with its stony soil. If you really want to see what that was like, go out and dig a two-by-two-by-two-foot hole, a pit barely big enough to support a post for a fence or a rural mailbox. Now imagine an excavation deep enough to put the footings below the frost line (that is, at least four feet deep here in southern New England) and wide enough to accommodate even a modest-sized house. My dad tells me my grandfather also dealt with rock ledges by hand. The workers would build fires on these stone outcroppings to heat them up and then pour cold water on them to crack the rock, before breaking it up and pulling it out by hand. After that, the men were free to mix the cement and sand and water in hand-cranked mixers and truck it over to the forms one wheelbarrow at a time, balancing the single wheel on concrete-spattered planks to get it to the top of the wall. Unbelievable. Building foundations is still hard work today, but in those days it was the work of titans.

"Form setter" is a modest title. I am not exactly sure why I am so proud of it, but I am, more so than if it had been "banker" or "lawyer," and even more than "doctor" or "professor." It speaks of hard work and honest labor yet encompasses the need for common sense and native intelligence, because if the foundation is not exactly as it should be—level and plumb, square and strong, waterproof—the rest of the building will never be right. It is one of the trades that built America and gave us the good life that many of us know but maybe take for granted. I suppose if I had been born in Iowa, it would have been farmer—or ranch hand if I were from Wyoming, logger if I were from Oregon. But I am from Massachusetts, and my dad was a form setter. I live the comfortable academic life today in large part because my father set forms, poured concrete, and built suburban homes through the cold and snow and the heat and humidity of thirty New England winters and summers.

And so my own story begins in suburbia, in an area that my father and grandfather helped build. It is one of the places that actually grew rapidly well before this most recent tidal wave of urbanization. Watertown was an early American suburb, a precursor to Levittown, New Jersey, and the post–World War II tract housing boom. Where you are from shapes who you are and marks you in some way for the rest of your life. Regardless of what I do and where I live now, I will always be at least partly a suburbanite. I, like the 20 percent of all Americans who move every year, have moved throughout much of my adult life.[12] Except for five years in the city of Tucson, all the places I've lived have been small towns, rural settings, or downright remote locations. I don't see myself now as a suburbanite, on the basis of profession or lifestyle. I would far prefer to raise chickens, spend the weekend cutting firewood, and have supper by the woodstove than go out on the town, attend a play, and have dinner at a fancy restaurant. I feel good knowing that there are wild turkeys and an abundance of deer in the backyard, and seeing a moose track in the streambed behind the house is an event of significance. My wife, Kiana, is from a small town in southern Wisconsin, but after spending twenty years in Alaska, she says southern Wisconsin is now too thickly settled for her to ever want to return. We now live in one of the more rural places I have ever lived, surprisingly enough right here in Western Massachusetts, and my aspiration is to have a closet full of nothing but blue jeans and flannel shirts and turn our place into a little farm. But my suburban beginnings mark me and have set me on a course that is etched into me, like my genetic background. My wife recognizes this and occasionally calls me "city boy."

Therefore, despite the criticisms that I can and will level at urbanization and the spread of suburbia, I have not distanced myself so far from it all as to forget that these cities and towns of ours are great places to live. Tucson is an example, with its mix of cultures, Southwestern architecture, and endless procession of sunny days. It is easy to understand why it has one of the fastest growth rates in the country, as more than two thousand people a month move there for the work and the warmth.[13] Boston is another good example. It is steeped in history and perched on the edge of the Atlantic. The beaches of Cape Cod, the coast of Maine, and the lakes of New Hampshire are not far away. There are more things to do in Boston—museums, concerts, nightclubs, restaurants, plays, and lectures—than a self-made hick like myself could even fathom, let alone take advantage of in a lifetime of trying. And there are many other examples of great cities here and around the world: Austin, Texas; Burlington, Vermont; Portland, Oregon; Madison, Wisconsin; Atlanta, Georgia; and Brisbane, Australia; Christchurch, New Zealand; and Amsterdam, London, and Rome. And great little towns, like Corvallis, Oregon; Flagstaff, Arizona; Moscow, Idaho; Barre, Massachusetts. Truth is, we mostly build pretty nice places to live, with all of the resources, services, and support that are so unfailingly available that it is easy to take it all for granted and focus on the crime, pollution, and poverty. This is not to say there isn't a lot of work to be done and improvement to be made in all these arenas; I just wonder whether we haven't become a society that overlooks the better things all around us every day because it is easy for so many of us to have so much.

So it would be hypocritical of me to talk of suburbia only as an evil place, growing like a cancer and sucking the life from the planet. Suburbia gave me a wonderful childhood with every opportunity. The work of my father—the suburban home builder; the attention of my mother—the suburban homemaker; and the company of my brothers and sisters and friends—most of whom are now raising families of their own in the suburbs—made it a safe and fun place to live. It was not and is not anywhere near perfect, but the suburbs of Boston, and I suspect of Chicago and Denver and Seattle and Atlanta and elsewhere, were and probably still are great places to live. Suburbia offers what most Americans, and as I hear many Australians and Canadians and Europeans and other people throughout the world, want: a home of their own, with a multicar garage and a manageable yard, all within easy distance of stores and services. Neighbors can at times be annoying, but the close proximity of others, in their nice homes with their messy garages and well-managed yards, makes us feel connected and safe. Most people don't see a need for twenty acres of woods with moose and turkeys in the backyard and wouldn't quite know what to do with them if they had them.

🐾 Washed by the fading light of early evening, a female coyote, in a blur of speed and blondish brown fur, dashes across the road and vanishes into the small patch of woods on the opposite side, melting into the brushy undergrowth. She is young, about a year and a half old, and on the move early. She is leaving the relative safety of her natal home for somewhere else. She hung on for a while in the place of her birth, assisting her mother in small ways with the raising of the next generation of pups. But the drought of late summer affected the availability of resources—no berries, no acorns, few rodents—and forced changes on her. Town managers required restaurant owners to clean up their dumpsters and encouraged homeowners to put lids on their trash barrels. Given the scarcity of food and the disturbance to some of the pack's usual haunts, it seemed a good time to leave. It is not important that she recognize why she is moving, or even be aware of where exactly she is going. The important thing is that she *is* moving, exploring new areas every day, searching for food every minute. She may wander like this for months or even years. The desire to be a nomad is always just under the surface when you are a coyote—but so is the drive to select a patch of ground and fulfill other deep-seated imperatives. It is a contradiction that shapes the breed and has served it well. For now, a narrow miss with the front end of a pickup truck was a good enough way to bid good-bye to daylight and welcome the beginning of a night of hunting.

We have already seen how adept coyotes as a species are at extending their geographic range. Humans not only killed off the coyotes' predators and competitors but also provided alternate sources of food. As soon as their frontiers expanded, in large part for these reasons, coyotes moved out in every direction from the Western prairies. Once established in a given area, coyotes can still range over fairly large tracts of land, and average about five square miles for adult males and about four for adult females. In northeastern North America, the size of their home range can vary from about seven to just over forty square miles. A coyote may defend all or part of its home range against other coyotes. This "land-tenure system of exclusive territories," as it has been called, can be maintained by direct confrontation with other coyotes or by more subtle (at least to us) means, such as scent-marking the boundaries and howling to advertise its presence.[14]

Lots of variables can influence the size of a coyote's territory, such as the gender of the individual, its social status, the season, the region of the geographic range, the local habitat, and, of course, food. The only determinant that can be considered typical is that there are not many set rules, as is in keeping with the coyote's character. Males generally claim larger territories than females, but not always. Packs of coyotes may have more extensive home ranges than coyotes living alone or in pairs, and territories are often larger in winter than summer.[15] When large carrion, like deer, are present in abundance, however, the home ranges of packs that defend the carcasses can be much more compressed than the range of loners or pairs. In the Northeast coyotes generally have somewhat bigger home ranges than in other parts of the country, and that is especially true in northern New England and eastern Canada, where animals are dealing with long, cold winters and deep snow.[16] Even there, give them a good winter with lots of deer or snowshoe hares, and all that will change.

Not a lot is known so far about the ecology of coyotes in urban or suburban areas, but we are slowly learning about it. Urban and suburban coyotes have been studied in places as disparate as Seattle, Los Angeles, Tucson, Jackson Hole, Chicago, and Cape Cod. Studies to date show that home range sizes vary in urban settings, from as little as half a square mile in LA to over forty-five square miles in Seattle. As you would expect, coyotes are just as adaptable in our neighborhoods as they are all over the continent. It is now true that the song dog of the prairie West has moved in next door in every state in the Union (except Hawaii) and is a full-time resident in the cities and towns of North America.[17]

CHAPTER 3

Gradient in Time
A Brief History of Wildlife in America

Slanted rays of the late-afternoon sun come in through the windows of the Cessna 206. I look to my left and see the glow on my wife's handsome face. She is smiling, looking down at the Okavango Delta in northern Botswana, southern Africa, which spreads out below us like God's own paradise. She is smiling because she has seen more species of ungulates in the last fifteen minutes than she has in the past several years: gemsbok and waterbuck, wildebeest and lechwe, puku, impala, and tsessebe. For every ungulate we have in North America, Africa must have at least five.[1] There are also families of elephants, gatherings of giraffes, occasional hippos. Moreover, not only is the number of species here fantastic, but there exists an incredible number of individuals of many of these species. The delta forms habitat for dozens of species of large mammals, countless species of birds, and myriad fish, amphibians, reptiles, invertebrates, and plants.

Water arrives from the north, coming slowly to the Okavango Delta. It gathers during the rainy season in the highlands of Angola until the land can hold no more and finally releases it in a large, shallow sheet, and the water creeps forward like dawn. By the time it makes it over the gentle terrain to northern Botswana, where it finds no outlet, several months have passed, and the dry season has arrived. And so by a miracle of nature and the combined forces of hydrology and gravity, the water floods thousands of square miles of land, creating a constellation of pools and islands at the driest time of year. Water brings life, and wildlife comes on wing or hoof to populate this vast region in numbers that inspire stories of an Eden on earth.

The plane banks. Ki looks over at me for a second and then back out the window, the smile on her face unchanging. Of many unique things about my wife, one is her special love of ungulates. As a wildlife biologist she has studied just about every species of ungulate on the North American continent: mountain goats and moose in Alaska, mule deer and pronghorn in Arizona, white-tailed deer in New England. As a biologist with the Alaska Department of Fish and Game, Kiana was something of a pioneer. She wasn't the first woman to work for the department, but she was a member of one of those early groups. Back when she was working in Anchorage, she started compiling data on encounters between humans and wildlife in the city. They were mostly calls from the public about errant moose and bears that had wandered into town, but Ki entered the information into a database she had created: who called, which species, where in town, what the problem was. Already in the early 1980s she was collecting data on urban wildlife, giving form and structure to a subdiscipline that did not yet have a widely recognized name. She did so because she was interested, she saw the need, and she knew it was a role that not many in the department would fulfill; most wanted to be working out of town, away from the public, chasing wolves and wolverines.

That suburban database still exists today, but Kiana's early role in its development has largely been forgotten. She offered this statement one day, as an observation, not a complaint. She has moved on to other things, always out in the field. In every encounter she has with the public, she explains in simple terms what she is doing and why it is important and why wildlife is a resource worth caring about.

We make one more round in the plane before heading back to town. The light is golden now, the shadows are long, and the fading sun glints off the water in flashes of silver. We see a small group of giraffes on the edge of a tree-covered island. They swing their heads skyward and then stand stock-still to watch us pass over, as graceful in stillness as they were in motion. The plane banks steeply as we turn to leave, and I watch the giraffes tilt away with the slanting of the earth.

It is the greatest of ecological understatements to remark that since the beginning of our existence we humans have been inextricably intertwined with the rest of life on the planet. We would not have come into being, nor would we continue to exist today, without the other life-forms—the fungi, plants, animals, and microbes, all the astonishing variety that we now call biodiversity—with which we share the earth.[2] I know that on some level we all realize this, yet somehow we think that now, in our modern era, we can do without many of those other species. It is an absurd idea that could only spring from a society that continually tries to insulate itself from the natural world. The fact is, little else is more important to our continued existence than biodiversity. We—who we are and what we are to become—are tied to the rest of life on earth.

Similarly, American history and society are connected in spirit and by circumstance to the natural world and the North American continent.[3] In the earliest days, humans roamed over the top of the world to reach the Western hemisphere. When they colonized a new world, they did so in the company of all the wild things that already lived here. The first people to arrive, who evolved into the original Americans, found a way to flourish, as they spread out from the Arctic to the tip of South America. It took resourcefulness and resiliency and a deep understanding of nature to attain that kind of success, and it is hard now to comprehend why we still talk about European colonization of America as the discovery of the continent. Whether these peoples truly lived in harmony with nature is for anthropologists and other scholars to debate. Given the natural abundance that filled the land and overflowed the shores of two continents, and the complex and varied societies of human inhabitants that Europeans found when they got here—it was a way of life perhaps as closely approaching harmony with nature as we can conceive. Surely the actions of indigenous people changed the landscape and the biota and extinctions and alterations took place in ecological communities, but by and large the Western hemisphere supported species and ecosystems of such diversity that if we could travel back in time, we would be dumbfounded at the beauty and bounty before us.

Europeans brought their views of nature with them when they landed on the shores of North America. But the continent presented the new arrivals with something for which few of them were prepared—a wilderness so vast and mysterious that it not only appeared limitless, but must also have been unimaginably intimidating. The challenge was to survive, establish a foothold, and eventually flourish in a new land filled with peril. Severe weather, wild animals, and defensive inhabitants were formidable and unforgiving antagonists. The promise of religious freedom must have paled in the face of harsh winters and impending starvation.

The first task at hand was to vanquish nature: establish a beachhead and hunker down for those first difficult years, carve out a farmstead, and secure the most basic requirements for all living things—water, food, and shelter. Once that battle was won, the further challenge was to tame nature to supply the settlers' remaining needs and wants: clear the woods, plow and sow the land, stock up for the coming winter, control the waterways to guard against flood or drought, and eradicate predators. Pioneers carried these aims westward as they recolonized the continent with a breed of people whose experience of nature derived from lands an ocean away. In Europe nature had been by and large tamed by the eighteenth century into terraces and rows and gardens. Wolves and bears still roamed some parts of the European continent, but they retreated to higher ground and into the inaccessible recesses of a landscape that had long felt the hand of domestication.

The watchwords of conquering and taming carried the nation well into the second century of its existence. In addition, another incentive strongly motivated early settlers: economics. The new Americans found themselves truly in a land of plenty. Fish, wildlife, timber, minerals, and land were available in such abundance that the only thing that outstripped them was the voracious appetite of the consumers. The growth in the national economy was driven largely by natural resources. Perhaps no other wildlife species illustrates the effects of the economic view of nature better than the beaver. The early economy of the colonies was largely dependent on the sale of pelts of beavers and other fur-bearing animals, such as fox, mink, otter, and lynx. Initially, colonists sold pelts to repay debts owed to European creditors. Then the huge demand in Europe for beaver felt hats fired the quest for beaver pelts, and it spread quickly over the entire geographic range of the species. The Hudson Bay Company was the largest and best-known exporter of furs. Although it kept excellent records, it is hard to determine just how many beaver pelts were shipped overseas.[4] Undoubtedly

the number ran into the millions. The boom lasted for the better part of two centuries before the fad for felt hats waned. By then beavers had been extirpated from much of their historic range.

Other wildlife was not immune to economic exploitation. In fact, just about every species that could be eaten or worn was subjected to what has been called market hunting. Hundreds of thousands of upland game birds, like sage grouse, ruffed grouse, sharp-tailed grouse, and prairie chickens, waterfowl, including just about all species of ducks and geese, and shorebirds were shot or trapped and plucked, cleaned, and shipped to markets throughout the eastern United States. Venison, elk meat, bison hump; bear, bison, and wolf hides; and the showy plumes of herons, egrets, and other birds all found their way to enthusiastic consumers in this country and abroad. Somehow, we managed to eradicate a continental population of passenger pigeons that may have numbered in the billions.[5] Several factors led to the demise of this once most abundant of species, but Americans actually ate many of them. Market hunting in no way resembles the sport hunting that we have today. In fact, it really should not be called hunting at all, and it is certainly not like subsistence hunting to feed yourself and your family or the sport hunting that is a managed form of recreation and a source of food for some. Market hunting was an all-out grab, unimpeded by limits, laws, or regulations of any kind.

Most people did not tolerate competition for the vast resources of the new continent in any form, and predators were seen not only as competitors but as major obstacles to amassing economic wealth and furthering the progress of civilization. We pursued and eradicated with extreme prejudice mountain lions, wolves, coyotes, foxes, bobcats, eagles, hawks, and anything else that ate the things we wanted. It may be hard these days to understand such slaughter. I can empathize with the people who were trying to eke out an existence and whose livestock were besieged by predators. Indeed, if you think that we can support our lifestyles today without some form of wildlife control, you are mistaken. Here, however, I am talking rather about the wholesale slaughter of predators because people just did not understand predator-prey interactions or the role of predation in the natural scheme of things. It's a prime example of our tendency to take extreme actions to deal with some issue without stopping to take a hard look at what we are doing and consider whether there might be another solution. Thousands of predators died because of our ignorance.

The day for reconsideration did in fact come. As much of the citizenry made money, and made merry over many a dinner of squab and venison steak, others were alarmed at the excesses of the market hunters and about the collective attitude toward natural resources. The best-known among these forward-thinking individuals were Theodore Roosevelt, John Muir, and Aldo Leopold. From the era of maximum exploitation came the first attempts to establish limits, regulations, and protective laws. Game management and conservation emerged out of mounds of deer skulls, piles of duck and grouse carcasses, and a profusion of plumes.

European laws had preserved wildlife for the use and amusement of royalty and the aristocracy. In the United States, though, the attitude that game and other natural resources were for the people superseded the European approach. The ability to subsist and make a living was the motivating factor in the early decades of the nation. The first game laws to regulate hunting through the setting of bag limits and season lengths came into existence in the States as early as the 1600s. The primary objective of these regulations was to maintain some semblance of sustainability for populations, so that the harvest of animals could continue. Throughout the late 1800s and most of the 1900s, game laws regulating sport hunting were a major factor in the successful preservation of habitat and restoration of wildlife populations. The publication of Aldo Leopold's *Game Management* (1933) marked the transformation of game management into a recognized profession.[6] Today, sport hunting and fishing are among the most highly regulated activities in the United States.

The first major federal wildlife law was the Lacey Act of 1900. In response to market hunting, the Lacey Act addressed, among other things, the prohibition on transporting across state lines game animals that had been taken (that is, killed) illegally. Other laws followed, such as the Migratory Bird Treaty Act of 1918, the Migratory Bird Hunting Stamp Act (the Duck Stamp Act) of 1934, and the Federal Aid in Wildlife Restoration Act (the Pittman-Robertson Act) of 1937, and later on its sister act, the Federal Aid in Sport Fish Restoration Act (the Dingell-Johnson Act) of 1950. The last three acts charged sport hunters and anglers either directly through stamp and license fees or indirectly, in the form of an excise tax on such sporting goods as guns, ammunition, and tackle. The vast majority of the sport hunting and fishing community encouraged and supported these acts, and the charging of fees and taxes. The funds quickly translated into game management efforts and into the purchase, protection, and restoration of lands for wildlife habitat. Today these funds play a major role in the conservation of all forms of wildlife, hunted or not.

Around the turn of the twentieth century, Americans were setting aside land for uses beyond subsistence or economic exploitation. Yellowstone became the first national park in 1872, the Forest Organic Act established the National Forest system in 1897, and Pelican Island in Florida became the first wildlife refuge in 1903. As the decades went by, more and more laws addressing all manner of environmental issues were added to the books: the Wilderness Act of 1964, the Clean Air Act and the National Environmental Policy Act (NEPA) of 1970, the Clean

tion of land and water and goods and energy are at their highest in our national lifespan, yet at the same time many Americans are confronting global climate change, depleted and degraded water supplies, sustainable forestry, livable cities, "green" building, recycling, and other issues—an active engagement that points to our increasing environmental awareness and maturation.

We are now becoming fully engaged in a relatively new phase of environmental awareness, urban ecology.[8] It recognizes that we as humans are a part of a planet that we have both inherited and influenced, to the point of creating ecosystems ourselves. Urban ecology deals with ideas like urban-rural gradients, suburban ecology, human ecology, the ecology of sprawl, the conservation of working landscapes, human-wildlife interactions and conflicts, and pest management. It examines the impact we as a people, through our actions—both positive and negative—have on the land and its wildlife.

Casual encounters with urban wildlife go a long way back. As soon as North America had towns and cities, it had some form of urban wildlife. Chimney swifts were known to nest in the chimneys of colonial homes as early as 1641.[9] No doubt some wildlife—raccoons, bats, deer mice, squirrels, wrens, robins, cardinals, wasps, spiders—was taking advantage of our homes and communities as soon as they were built.

In the early 1900s researchers began publishing findings on wildlife in towns and cities.[10] These first papers focused on birds and emphasized the use of artificial nest boxes and birdfeeders and the use of gardens and landscaping to attract songbirds. During the mid-1900s studies began to show up about the distribution of birds and mammals, such as squirrels and opossums, in developed areas. Interest in attracting birds to city parks and suburban backyards grew. The general attitude was that wildlife was desirable and that birds and their presence, in particular, enriched the lives of city dwellers and town residents. People recognized that living in proximity to wildlife bestowed certain social and economic benefits. Still, the ornithologist W. Erz wrote in 1966, "studies of the artificial habitats of towns and cities seem to be no popular subject of real 'nature' study."[11]

Despite that comment, in the 1960s such studies were initiated in cities all over the world—Brussels, Hong Kong, Tokyo, Sydney, and Rome, among others. By investigating the structure and natural processes of the urban environment, and the ways in which humans fit into and live in it, these studies laid a strong foundation for urban ecology. Later on, the United Kingdom, the United States, and Germany undertook long-term research in urban areas.

General interest in urban wildlife grew during the 1970s, and for a while it even became a hot topic. Professional biologists and managers held meetings to discuss related issues, and bibliographies and proceedings of several large conferences were published, with such titles as *Wildlife in an Urbanizing Environment, Man and Nature in the City, Wildlife in Urban Canada,* and *An Annotated Bibliography on Planning and Management for Urban-Suburban Wildlife.*[12] Papers covered the ecology of the urban environment, the effects of urbanization on wildlife populations, plantings for wildlife, animal damage control, and issues related to human health and welfare. The emphasis was still largely on attracting birds, but dozens of papers discussed other species, such as butterflies. Many articles portrayed the positive aspects of attracting wildlife, but some were beginning to focus on what has come to be called problem wildlife.

Despite the proliferation of symposia and published proceedings on urban/suburban wildlife during the 1970s, the wildlife profession seemed to lose interest in the topic in the 1980s.[13] It may have been seen as not serious enough, or maybe other issues were more important or pressing. My belief is that controversies such as the conflict over spotted owls and logging of old-growth forest dominated the conservation arena. At the heart of the issue lay the rate, intensity, and extent of logging in the remaining old-growth forests of the Pacific Northwest, particularly when that logging involved large clear-cuts (a timber-harvesting technique where every stem is removed). Among the concerns was what the cumulative loss of old growth might mean for the continued existence of spotted owls and other species that relied on that habitat. Biologists, conservation organizations, land managers, politicians, and the media focused intensely on the controversy, which was reduced (unfortunately and inaccurately) to "jobs versus owls." The northern spotted owl was listed as a threatened species under the Endangered Species Act during this time. The listing afforded the owl more protection, while at the same time effectively limiting some timber harvest. Thus the listing sharpened the focus on job losses in the timber industry and economic losses in the region. The Endangered Species Act was examined by Congress as never before, and the debate over its continued existence and effectiveness spread from the Northwest to other parts of the nation. Because of the public and political scrutiny, including a summit that brought the president of the United States to Portland, Oregon, to preside over the meeting, the spotted owl controversy has been called a watershed topic in conservation.[14] Eyes were focused on this and similar issues during the 1980s, a time when few people saw urban wildlife as a subject of much relevance.

As we moved into the 1990s, the topic came to be among those most studied by researchers and one of tremendous concern to managers in the wildlife profession. Published literature on the subject grew astronomically, and state agencies like the Massachusetts Division of Fisheries and Wildlife (MassWildlife, for short) developed programs devoted to urban wildlife and hired staff to work in this area. Wildlife professionals became much more aware of the importance of the human element in all aspects of wildlife ecology, and many experts became versed in matters relating to policy, stakeholder involvement, health and human safety, human-wildlife interactions, and other aspects of human dimensions, as it is now known. My friend and colleague Rob Deblinger is an example of this new breed of wildlife professional. Rob got his Ph.D. from Colorado State University while studying pronghorn that range across the open plains of southern Wyoming. He is now a deputy director at MassWildlife. He has created an urban and suburban emphasis within his agency, and he is as fully engaged in matters of policy and human-wildlife interactions as he is in biology.[15] Many university departments in fisheries and wildlife, conservation biology, and natural resources studies have a program emphasis and courses in urban ecology. Most major professional ecological societies deal with the subject in their journals, on their Web sites, and at their annual meetings. It is a topic that has grown faster than any other I have witnessed in my profession so far.

The relatively new emphasis on urban ecology is a good one for our society. The field merges two sets of concerns: the human element and all that it represents, and the natural world. The focus, which is on the way we live in and relate to the ecology of our planet, draws attention to the things we do right and the mistakes we continue to make.

In general, coyotes search for food everywhere, and the young female is no different. Her suburban surroundings offer many opportunities, and she is always ready to take advantage of the circumstances. So when a rabbit ventures out away from the brush pile that lies decomposing in a corner of a vacant lot, she notices and watches. The rabbit has been gnawing away at the tender bark of some brushy growth that the town's landscaping crew missed. Too late, the rabbit realizes that eating has occupied too much of its attention, and before it has time to make it halfway back to cover, the coyote is upon it. Only the jays hear the brief but piercing scream, and they gather overhead to harass the female as she trots off with her prize.

The female coyote is out doing what she does best, finding food. Coyotes are by classification and phylogeny carnivores, predators and hunters, used to eating flesh; their success in both distribution and numbers in North America is evidence that they are good at that occupation. But in practice they are omnivores, from *omni-*, meaning "all," and *vorare*, meaning "to eat greedily." In real life, coyotes, just like humans, will eat practically anything and everything.

In several publications on coyote diet, the following items have been identified as being eaten by coyotes: mice, voles, birds, reptiles, beetles, other insects and other invertebrates, berries (including blackberries, blueberries, raspberries, huckleberries, serviceberries, and shadberries), vegetables, eggs, pikas, jackrabbits, snowshoe hares and cottontails, mule deer, white-tailed deer, pronghorn, ground squirrels, tree squirrels, cotton rats, pocket gophers, domestic sheep, domestic cats, small domestic dogs, cattle, chickens, pigs, goats, watermelons, persimmons, wild grapes, wild plums, porcupines, badgers, chipmunks, woodchucks, grouse, ducks, muskrats, shrews, flying squirrels, red fox, wild cherries, apples, beechnuts, raccoons, garbage, dog food, cat food, and moose carrion.[16]

I am sure there is more, but you get the idea. Coyotes have a diverse diet. Unfortunately for them, several of the things they like to eat have created controversy and given them a negative reputation in certain quarters. A predilection for lambs and calves has given the coyote a lot of bad press over the years, some of it deserved. The fact that coyotes will eat deer has also gotten them into trouble. Some deer hunters, particularly in the northeastern United States and eastern Canada, don't like the idea of coyotes' moving in and competing with them for big game. It is true coyotes can kill a fair number of deer, especially during the winter, when conditions are right (for the coyotes, not the deer). Some biologists who have been studying coyotes and deer for quite a while, however, believe that the relation between coyote predation and numbers of deer is too complex for us to be able to attribute declines in the deer population merely to the ravages of coyotes. Coyotes do take deer, but predator-prey interactions, involving such factors as weather, terrain, and food resources, are generally way too complex for us to blame a population downturn on a single cause.

The coyotes' problem actually gets worse in the suburbs. For one thing, coyotes will sometimes eat domestic cats. On occasion they chase them down, grab them, shake them, and consume them like any tender wild rabbit. The same fate can befall little dogs. I know that some people find it offensive even to discuss it, but it does happen. One solution is not to let your cat roam free; predators will not be able to get your cat, and your cat will not be out killing wildlife. No one really knows how many domestic cats are killed by coyotes, but when a cat turns up missing nowadays, it is often a coyote that gets blamed. I am sure that domestic dogs, other cats, fishers, great horned owls, automobiles, human subadults with a twisted sense of fun, and human adults who have a bone to pick with cats play a role in cat mortality, but the coyote is the one that takes the fall.

Recent studies show that a large part of the coyote diet in urban and suburban areas comprises such small mammals as voles and mice, animals that top the list of pests.[17] Cats and garbage actually form a very small part of that diet.

For all the trouble that coyotes get into, the fact that they have, although very rarely, attacked people puts them in a whole new light. Rabies can make animals do irrational things, and rabid coyotes have been known to come after humans, even adults, and bite them. That is one thing, but the very idea of a coyote snatching a young child from the backyard is a horror we can hardly comprehend. It is an unlikely event to be sure, and far, far rarer than attacks on children by domestic dogs, but in the few cases when we do hear of it, we recoil in terror.

Wild-animal attacks on humans are really quite rare, and the fatalities that Americans suffer in vehicle accidents, assaults, falls, drownings, and other accidents far outweigh wildlife-related fatalities, which are, at least statistically, insignificant. About forty-eight thousand people, for example, die each year in automobile accidents, thirty-one thousand by suicide, seventeen thousand from human assaults, sixteen thousand from falls, thirty-five hundred from drowning, and three thousand in fires. Of the human deaths caused by the animal kingdom, most are actually allergic reactions to insect stings or spider bites (about sixty a year). The tally for human deaths due to larger animals is so low that it needs to be counted over multiple years—for example, about two people killed by black bears and four or five by grizzlies every ten years. Compare this figure to the fifteen to twenty Americans killed every year by domestic dogs.[18]

We need to be educated about the ways of coyotes, and we should place the highest priority on the protection of children who might be vulnerable to attack. We also have to take a clear look at the real situation, though, and deal with it in rational ways.

I have never really understood why dog attacks on kids don't have more of an impact on society, given that they happen far more often than any attacks by wildlife. I do understand, however, why one or two cases of coyote attacks on children do catch people's attention. The coyote is a wild animal, beyond our control, and the idea of this wild creature lurking around the yard and looking at our young children as a potential source of food conjures up nearly forgotten and long-repressed memories of our original place in nature. Sharks, bears, lions, cougars, and tigers elicit the same gut response. It is a fear that lies deep inside, the knowledge on some level that we are prey for animals that are bigger, faster, and stronger than we are. Most of us never have to really worry about this threat, but remote as it remains, it is a shock to our system. It poses an unacceptable challenge to our worldview and our sense of ourselves as masters of all we survey.

CHAPTER 4

Suburban Wildlife Encounters

The windswept tundra lies ahead, an endless plain shrouded in fog and cold. It is early June, but a late spring storm has moved in, producing a mix of snow and sleet that blows in sideways from the north and west. The visibility is reduced to about forty feet, and everything is covered with a crystalline shell of crusty snow. The whole scene gives the land an air of mystery and impenetrability that serves only to beckon us farther into it.

There are eight of us in all, biologists from Manitoba and Minnesota, Missouri and Arkansas and Wisconsin, different parts of the Mississippi Flyway—that broad strip of land that commands the near-center of the continent, defined and named by the river that traverses most of it from north to south. We are loosely aligned in a broad front as we move into the fog and freezing sleet, looking for Canada geese huddled on their clutches of eggs. The females are determined to sit tight on their nests no matter what the weather or the disturbance, to protect their precious unhatched young against anything that might harm them.

Lost to one another except for the occasional dim outline marked by hunched shoulders and a deliberate pace, we move forward in a broken line as we look for the nesting birds. We record the location when we spy the nests, but we back off then, to avoid making the geese stand and flee. We'll leave them be for today and wait for better weather to count the clutch and candle the eggs.

The ground is spongy underfoot, the sleet stinging, and I think of hikes I have taken in warmer places by the shores of oceans that are not frozen at this time of year. But I am comfortable in my protective shell of wool and Gore-Tex. I can no longer see my companions to the left and right, and the wind is loud enough and the fog thick enough that I feel I may be the only person now walking at the top end of the world.[1] My binoculars are fogged over, to the point of being nearly useless, but I can see a small group of caribou pass near me in a confusion of legs and antlers. They hold their heads high and pump their legs in the way of caribou on the move. They come toward me, they pass, and then they are lost in the whiteness as suddenly as they appeared.

Marin County, California, is a sunny place. The people are sunny, too, with tans and sunny dispositions. They drive nice cars and live in nice homes. Many of the homes have very nice views of San Francisco Bay and the bridges that cross the bay, of the grassy green hills dotted with live oaks and eucalyptus trees that rim the bay, and of the other nice homes with their nice views of the bay and the bridges and the hills and the other houses. It's nice.

The people in the upscale grocery market at the base of the hills, nestled into a spot along the bay, are very friendly. They make eye contact with you and inquire if they can help. When you ask them something, like "Where can I find the Punjab choley?" they look up and smile and actually take you to where the Punjab choley is. They wish you a good day as if they mean it. The market is crowded and the lines are long, but you leave not feeling stressed. You almost enjoyed the experience and don't mind waiting and paying the prices. It is pleasant, and it is enough to make a cynical native New Englander wary and a bit edgy. Is this place real? Are these people real? Does it ever get cold or rain here? I try not to like what I see, and I make some half-hearted, disparaging remarks to my wife as we make our way back to the car with our bundles of wine and flowers and groceries, but I think, I do kind of like this, and if I ever lived here maybe I could be like one of them, swept up body and soul in the sunny California lifestyle.

Of course, Californians have their confrontations with reality, too. A major highway overpass just melted and collapsed when a tanker truck crashed and exploded yesterday. Rallies are planned to protest immigration laws in all the major metropolitan areas today. The residents of Los Angeles and San Francisco just learned that their cities are among the most polluted in the country. And if it doesn't rain soon, the state will experience another savage fire season that seems to get longer, hotter, and more intense every year.

I am mulling these things over again as I hike now through the hills just above the town. It is pleasant up on the high ground, and I think of the times I have spent at higher latitudes, where inclement weather dominates and warm days are rare. There must have been some rain here, or at least adequate amounts of early morning coastal fog, because the grass and the coyote brush are very green. I move through the shade of an oak grove and emerge near the top of the hill. The view *is* nice. I look down at all of the houses and condominiums, and I can hear the traffic noise rising like hot air from the low ground. Despite the pretty views, this place is busy and crowded. There are many ways to deal with crowded conditions. One way is to avert your eyes and act introverted, suspicious of people's intentions and cynical about their motives and actions. The other is to be pleasant and polite, maybe even overly so, and face the crowds with that sunny smile and a heartfelt "Have a nice day." Neither form of behavior is perhaps entirely normal for our species, but either may be a reaction to the overcrowding we are experiencing just about everywhere.

Given the circumstances and the times we live in, I find myself favoring the Californians' approach. Maybe someday I *could* live here, adopting a more pleasant attitude, trading in my blue jeans and flannel shirts for pastel-colored shorts and a T-shirt with flowers on it, volunteering to show people where to find the Punjab choley. Maybe I need to practice this friendlier, more open approach on New Englanders when I get home. The thought makes me smile.

I look down at the trail as I continue my hike and realize something else. This place is covered with coyote poop. The droppings are everywhere, ranging in color from black to bleached-out white. They are twisted and gnarly, the way coyote scats tend to be, and I can see protruding bits of bone and tufts of hair. Some scat is riddled with berry seeds. Occasionally a piece of trash, maybe a plastic wrapper, is mixed up in it.

Experience and research have shown field biologists that the amount of scat is not necessarily a good index to the number of animals, whether deer or rabbits or quail or coyotes. There are too many variables that can influence the distribution and abundance of scat and the rate at which it disintegrates—among them diet, weather conditions, and animal behavior such as territoriality. At any rate, there is a lot of coyote poop in these hills, and I am thinking there are a lot of coyotes, too.

It seems, then, that this is one of the many places where the world of suburbanites and the world of coyotes intersect. People down in those nice houses have no doubt seen coyotes, as well as black-tailed deer, foxes, raccoons, skunks, turkeys, many different kinds of songbirds, and other critters in their neighborhoods. When the residents see a coyote, hear a rumor of a bobcat, or read another newspaper article about cougars, they worry at times about their kids', their pets', and their own personal safety.

A fair bit of wildlife lives up here, and it leads me to wonder how these two worlds merge—our tame and tidy suburban environment and the unrestricted and untended hills and ravines that harbor wild animals. Ki and I have seen only a few people in a week of hiking, so not a lot of locals venture up into these somewhat wilder areas; a few joggers and mountain bikers have constituted our only human sightings. Most times we have the place to ourselves. I wonder if it is just the lack of time that keeps most people away, or a nagging fear that something wicked may occupy this pretty, rolling terrain so close to home.

News of wildlife run-ins with people is common in California. The more serious the encounter, of course, the more newsworthy, so these are the stories that receive the most coverage. When a mountain lion jumped a woman who was hiking along a trail in central California, and then tried to drag her off by her face until her companions forced the cougar into flight by stabbing it and pelting it with rocks, we all heard about it. The same holds true across the continent: a coyote attacked an older couple on a hiking trail in Massachusetts, and the woman fought the animal off and then ran and got help for her husband.[2] Attacks on pets and people, including children, by cougars and coyotes and foxes and raccoons and bears are really not common, but they don't have to be. When an attack does occur, we want to hear about it. Professional biologists (including me) sometimes deride the media for emphasizing the negative, making big news out of rare events, encouraging our tendency to stare at accidents—like rubbernecking when we pass a car wreck on the highway—but after all, it is human nature. We look with morbid fascination and curiosity at such stories, especially when a wild animal is involved. I am sure we have been doing this forever, ever since we sat up in the trees thousands of years ago, watching in horror as a leopard dragged off and devoured one of our clanmates. I am not making light of it. I am saying that attacks by wild, free-ranging animals on humans are all at once rare, unlikely, scary, and disturbing.[3] But when they do happen we want to look on at a safe distance.

The other reports on encounters between humans and wildlife that tend to make the news are the comical ones. In the police log in a local newspaper near my hometown a woman reported a large, hairy man swimming in her pool in the middle of the night. The large, hairy man turned out to be a large, hairy black bear, which left the scene peacefully as soon as it had enough of the chlorinated water. In Alaska, moose enter people's yards and leave with Christmas lights, laundry, or tire swings affixed to their antlers. Wild turkeys are sometimes reported chasing people around their cars, and let's admit that the image of a tom turkey chasing a businessman around his Volvo is pretty humorous. Every year we hear about the people who think they have a burglar or worse in their house, only to find out that a raccoon or skunk has made it in through the pet door. Thus it is the tragedies and the comedies of our interactions with wild animals that tend to capture our attention, and perhaps this combination further defines our evolving relationship with nature.

It is often reported in both the scientific and popular media that the frequency of encounters between human beings and wild animals is on the rise. Maybe so. It is true these types of stories are currently very newsworthy. They are proliferating in print, on television, and on the Internet.

I do wonder, though, whether the number of such encounters is really growing. Do we run into wildlife more frequently than did people of generations past, who led a more rural existence? It is certainly true that there are a lot more people now than there were a few decades ago, but are we really sharing our space with more animals, or is it just that when we do see that raccoon or skunk or deer in the yard, it is more of an event? Has it reached a point where almost any sighting of almost any wild animal is newsworthy?

Ki tells me that she has gotten several reports from people who have seen black bears in the Quabbin watershed in central Massachusetts, where she works as the area biologist. When they call, she asks if the bear was being aggressive or threatening.

No has always been the answer so far.

"So what was it doing?" she asks, to which the caller replies something like, "It was just standing there, and then moved off into the woods." Or, "As soon as it saw us, it took off running."

So Ki will tell them thank you for the report and congratulations on seeing one of the Quabbin's most charismatic residents.

But it doesn't end there. They invariably ask, "Shouldn't something be done?"

"What would you like us to do?" she asks politely.

"I don't know. Come out and dart it or something. We just thought someone should know."

It is a bear out in the woods that happened to be seen by some people, but more and more often our reaction seems to be that something needs to be done about it. Ki tells the callers never to approach a bear when they see one, and never, ever to offer one food, and that by and large it will just keep about its business and that should be the end of it. Certainly bears can be aggressive at times, and they may appear unpredictable if you are not familiar with their behavior. Otherwise, a bear in the woods is not particularly unusual, and I hope it never will be. I am not sure everyone understands it the same way, however.

Part of the reason that the frequency of human-wildlife encounters seems to be growing everywhere in the country is that we are moving farther and farther into wildlife habitat.[4] When you build your home up in the hills of California or the foothills of the Colorado Rockies, or out in the desert around Tucson or Las Vegas, or farther into the woods of Massachusetts and Maine, you are going to increase your encounters with wildlife. We are moving in greater numbers out into what was once mostly wildlife habitat, and for a while, at least, we will be sharing that space with other species.

Another reason for the apparent increased frequency of human-wildlife encounters is that many forms of wildlife have either adapted quite well to our built environment or are predisposed to do just fine in it.[5] They find all the resources they need and all the conditions that make our hometowns their habitat. Not every creature reacts to human development this way, but many of them do, and so we find ourselves living with wildlife. If animals are already there, they stay. If they have been absent from the area for a while, they are attracted to the amenities the suburban environment has to offer: the basic requirements of food, water, shelter from the elements, and protection from predators that spell habitat for any given species.

Still another possible reason for increased human-wildlife interactions is the learned behavior of many species. Most if not all species are pretty adaptable and have a great capacity for learning. The strongest stimulus to learning may be experience, and the most basic motivation fear.[6] So, for example, when you chase bears and mountain lions with hounds, they learn to avoid people. Hunting, like other forms of predation, makes animals wary, and as a result prowling around backyards and in neighborhoods that smell of humans and their pets may not seem like a good idea to creatures that know what the consequences might be. Animals learn quickly what is hazardous and what is not. I have seen geese fly out of a refuge by first circling and gaining altitude and then flying high over the line of hunting blinds that ring the border of the reserve. The geese come back in the same way: way up in the air they return from feeding in the surrounding fields, until the birds know they are past the shooting line and up over the refuge. Only then do they descend in long spirals to the safety of the protected marshes.

When we outlaw or limit activities such as hunting, some species either lose their fear of humans or, in the case of young individuals, never develop it. As a consequence you see the bold behavior of some mountain lions and bears and coyotes on the edge of suburbia and within its borders. It doesn't matter to me whether you are in favor of hunting or whether the very thought of it repulses you: the fact is that as we alter our behavior, animals alter theirs, too.

Another thing about our handling of encounters between humans and wildlife is that many, if not most, of the stories about them focus on the negative. Our society is beginning to regard more and more species of wildlife as problems and pests. We seem to have an underlying belief that wildlife threatens us directly, through potential attacks, or indirectly, through potential disease (Lyme disease, rabies, or avian flu, to name a few). If not that, animals are out to damage our property, get into our garbage, steal our pets' food, leave droppings on our lawns, get hit by cars, and otherwise create problems.[7] We like animals—after all, we feed birds and photograph animals and subscribe to dozens of wildlife magazines and watch Animal Planet—but there are limits to what we will tolerate. When animals overstep those boundaries, we want swift action and an immediate response to our problems, whether they are real or perceived.

In short, we have developed a dichotomous response to wildlife.[8] We tend to label some wildlife as good and some as bad. Any songbird or butterfly is almost invariably good. Almost any kind of rodent or biting insect is invariably bad. Most species can be good or bad, however, depending on our circumstances and their behavior. We like beavers when there are not too many of them and they create their nice ponds in the right places. We hate them with a passion as their numbers grow and they flood our roads and septic systems or gnaw down our prized trees. Canada geese are handsome and entertaining, especially when they have goslings, but they defecate more than almost any vertebrate alive, and those greasy green droppings in our parks and on our golf courses and lawns are disgusting to most people. The coyote is always interesting. In the last few years we have developed a new appreciation and admiration for predators, but there will always be something about the coyote that makes us a bit uneasy. We may like the idea of the coyote, but I am not sure how much we really like the animal itself.

Biologists believe that, over the long term, animal populations tend to hover at, around, or just below "carrying capacity." Carrying capacity is a concept that defines how many animals the environment, with all its essential resources of food, water, and shelter (as well as other factors, such as individuals with which to mate), can sustain. When animal numbers exceed biological carrying capacity, the population will decline to a level that can be maintained. In the case of species such as deer and moose that can actually deplete their own food supplies, the level at which the numbers can be maintained may now be much lower than it was previously, because of the impact of the species on their own habitat.

When animal populations get above some level that is called cultural carrying capacity (or which some human-dimensions specialists term stakeholder acceptance level), the animals are labeled overabundant.[9] All this really means is that there are too many of them for our liking. For many species, cultural carrying capacity is almost always at a lower level than biological carrying capacity—that is, the number of creatures we can tolerate is lower than the number the environment can sustain.

At the same time, however, society is rejecting the idea of population control through such means as hunting and trapping.[10] We don't want these animals killed by hunters and trappers for meat and fur. Rather, we see the issue as one of pest management, so we hire professional exterminators to remove the unwanted critters from our presence. These individuals are then disposed of as garbage, thrown in the dump or in a ditch. By virtue of our desire to protect them from hunting and trapping, we disregard the fact that the populations of these species will grow, often exponentially. When they do, our response is to designate them as unwanted nuisances and get someone to do the dirty work and keep the results from our view. Another, often unreported, consequence of this situation is that some people take matters into their own hands. No local trapper or group of hunters comes around anymore to take some animals during a designated, legal harvest season. In addition, hiring a pest management professional can be expensive, and the new regulations governing pest control are often cumbersome. So the alternative is to go out and deal with the problem yourself, by whatever means possible. Those means are likely to be unregulated and unreported, sometimes inhumane, and they usually put the landowner or property owner in an untenable situation. A balance needs to be struck between appreciating and tolerating wildlife, on the one hand, and controlling their numbers when matters of public health and safety and ecosystem integrity are involved, on the other.

In many states the decision about the best way to deal with wild populations is made by voter referendum, and a clear division often exists between those who dwell in towns and cities and those who live in rural areas. In fact, in an interesting case in Massachusetts involving a referendum on fur trapping (and other issues), researchers found a threshold at a density of four hundred people per square mile, above which almost all towns voted to ban the use of foothold (and other body-gripping) traps, and below which most people voted to retain the use of these traps.[11] In this case, a pretty clear difference existed, based on population density, between towns—a metric that is often used to distinguish between "rural" and "urban." The urban/suburban view of the world tends to predominate over the rural view because people in the urban areas greatly outnumber those in rural areas in many if not most states.

Such voter referendums usually lead to further regulation and more restrictions. Thus, a dominant and growing tendency exists in American society toward preservation, and the concept or even the term "natural resources" has become offensive to some because it connotes human use. Similar feelings apply to fisheries, forest, and range management as well.

I am reporting this more than criticizing it, but with one cautionary note. When overdone, extreme opinions about preservation can lead to our actually separating ourselves from nature rather than drawing closer. It can create a kind of a museum or zoo mentality that leads us to say: "Here we are . . . and there is Nature over there. We are not a part of Nature, so stay out and leave it alone." Preservation does play a major role in conservation, but we need to think about the implications of playing only that one card. What does it mean when we allow none of the traditional uses of natural resources? Is there a place for working landscapes in and among our communities and in the matrix of land around our reserves? Can those who hunt and fish rally to the defense of nature alongside those who hike and go birdwatching?[12] If not, I fear that our divisions will get the best of us in the constant struggle for conservation.

Society's views toward wildlife are always changing, and there may be no better example of this than our attitudes toward the mountain lion, or cougar.[13] When I was a young man working in the Cascade Mountains of north-central Washington State, I met an old lion hunter. It was during the 1980s and I was as young as he was old. His heyday had been in the middle of the twentieth century, during the 1940s and 1950s, when he was the top bounty hunter in the region. He showed me dozens of articles, each of which detailed the accounts of his hunts and documented his successes with photographs of dead lions draped over the hood of his vehicle. The entire town would turn out to see the return of the hunter and his prize. It was obvious from our discussions that at one time the lion hunter was a person of renown and importance in the community.

In the 1960s our perception of mountain lions was beginning to change, largely because of a man named Maurice Hornocker.[14] Hornocker's research presented the mountain lion in a heretofore unfamiliar light, and such themes as the balance between populations of predators and prey, and predators as an integral part of natural ecosystems, echoed throughout Hornocker's work and that of other biologists. The mountain lion was also promoted as a trophy animal rather than as a pest to be killed for bounty, thus effectively bringing it under the protection of state and federal game laws and providing local game agencies with a method for controlling numbers.

By the 1980s and 1990s, attitudes changed again. Large predators like mountain lions had achieved a new status. Beyond the simple recognition of their role as top carnivores, people experienced an almost spiritual awakening or personal connection with predators. For many, the idea that large predators like cougars and bears might be defined as game species and thus subjected to recreational hunting was abhorrent. Many urbanites who had moved into the growing cities of Western states like Arizona, California, Colorado, and Idaho did not like the idea of lion hunting, and especially did not like the idea of lion hunters using hounds to chase and tree cougars before shooting them. Hounds were also used to hunt bears and bobcats. In states that had voter referendums, the question of banning hunting with hounds was put on the ballot and it was an easy win. Thus the mountain lion was now viewed as a species deserving total protection by the urban/suburban majority.

More recently, mountain lions and people have entered a new era of human-wildlife interactions. As people have built their homes and pursued their recreational activities in larger numbers and farther into lion habitat, unprovoked attacks on humans have increased.[15] Although the number of such incidents is still small, awareness and concern are mounting. Some members of society now view lions as a threat to human safety, and along with that perception comes the demand that someone protect us.

Thus, in the course of half a century or so the mountain lion has gone from pest to game species to wilderness icon to threat to human health and safety. If attacks on humans continue, many segments of the public will demand that the problem be addressed, and the language used to convey the message may not be very different from that of livestock growers in the early part of the twentieth century. If development continues to encroach on lion habitat, the problem may eventually go away of its own accord, when cougar populations are wiped out altogether. Either way, the end result will not be anything most wildlife professionals or concerned members of the public would deem a positive outcome.

A howl pierces the early evening, shrill as an alarm clock shattering the morning silence, and right away a chorus of yips and yowls joins in, in the pleasure of making noise. The young female hears it, but already aware of the presence of others, she is moving away, putting another row of houses between her and the pack. She covers ground quickly, navigating down an alley, skirting backyards. She pauses briefly to sniff at a bowl sitting on the edge of a deck. It is empty, but she takes a second to lick the bottom and sides a few times before hurrying on. She sniffs at the base of a tree, long since dry but carrying a message nonetheless. She has seen and smelled and heard enough now and proceeds on her way.

Chief among the characteristics of the coyote that lend themselves to legend, myth, and story is their voice.[16] Coyotes communicate in many different ways, but they are really known for their calls—the yips, yaps, yowls, and howls that are the spirit of the Western plains and deserts and now fill Eastern woodlands like mist and infiltrate urban and suburban settings.

It is that voice which reaches us across the darkness and reminds us that we share the earth with others. People of earlier times would have said that coyotes can tell you things, if you know how to listen. Legend has it that coyotes can predict whether you will have a good day, or whether today is the day you will meet your death. They can show you what to eat or direct you to water. They will warn you about the approach of others and let you know if they are friend or foe. They can talk their way through barbed-wire fences and forecast rain or a change in the weather. Coyotes can speak Comanche, Apache, Navajo, and several other Native American languages. After some time they learned Spanish (Mexican dialects, of course, and not Castilian) but apparently never could get through to English speakers. Anyway, that is how the stories go. It has also been said that all coyotes are liars, but perhaps they have merely learned to tell others only what they want to hear. That would be a logical adaptation for a creature whose main goal is to survive in a world where not everyone plays fair.

Coyotes communicate with each other through scent as well as sound. Much of the communication is contained in urine; both males and females deposit their scent in select spots throughout their territory, to advertise their presence and respond to the messages of others. When the animals are together in packs or family groups, visual cues offer a wealth of indicators. Curled lips and bared canines unmistakably show aggression. Flattened-down ears and a drooping tail indicate submission; rolling over on the back is a sign of extreme submission. Legs splayed out, front end down, and rear end up are an invitation to play. Some of these visual signals are obvious, some subtle. Several you can see in your pet dog.

But it is the vocal repertoire of the coyote that carries its messages the furthest and plays into our images and imaginings of the wild. So what might coyotes be telling us modern people who are in constant communication with one another, to the point where we have little time for messages from nature? Maybe it is just that they are here. Maybe they show us that we have much more in common with them than we think. Maybe we can consider their message to be simply that they like these urban and suburban areas of ours just fine, and that they might like to stay awhile, regardless of our opinion on the matter.

CHAPTER 5

Mixed Messages

🐾 I have mixed feelings about being back in Massachusetts. After so many years in the West I had missed the New England landscape and my family. I wanted to get back to my roots. I constantly thought about the seasons—the colors of fall, the snow in winter, spring coming on, summer lush and green. So much of the West is dry that I found myself dreaming of water. By the time I did come back east, though, a vision of open vistas and larger spaces had left indelible marks on my memory. I had gotten used to the lower density of people in places west of the 100th meridian. I had come to take great comfort in the idea that national forests and national parks were abundant and never very far away, no matter how much we all argue about the concept of public lands and fuss over how we manage them.

I worry about the concentration of people here in Massachusetts, the number of roads, the ceaseless encroachment of development, and maybe most of all the alarming nonchalance of many of the state's residents toward the spread of the built environment. It is a mind-set that brings people to believe that an area like the watershed of the Quabbin Reservoir is wilderness. It may be true that wilderness is in the eye, heart, and mind of the beholder, but at some point one needs to face the music. I love the Quabbin: I like working landscapes and the sense of history, and I admire the great job the people who manage the watershed do in the face of many different pressures, but the people of Massachusetts have not known the solace of true wilderness for many generations.

That is why it came as a surprise when I first heard that moose—maybe as many as a thousand or more individuals—inhabited the state. Two or three decades ago most people would have been suspicious of any supposed sighting of a moose in Massachusetts, but these largest members of the deer family are back in force, strolling in from the north on long legs. I took this to be more than a fortunate twist of fate: it was a good omen, a ray of hope. If we had room for moose in Massachusetts, all might not be lost after all.

I didn't know how long it would take me to see my first moose in Massachusetts. I had been back here in New England for five years and I had been out and about, up and down streams, over wooded ridges, into beaver haunts and down country roads—still no moose. I had seen tracks and discovered droppings, found bent and broken saplings and signs of browsing on winter buds—all the clues a moose will leave behind—but not one glimpse of an animal.

We had been living in the state no more than two years before Ki saw her first moose—not much gets past her when she is in the woods—but no moose for me. I didn't say much about it, just kept up my silent watch and waited for the day when I could come home and say, "Guess what I saw today?"

I had seen lots of moose before, in Maine and New Hampshire and Alaska and Wyoming. They are huge and impressive no matter where you see them. Many people think moose look funny or weird, with those big noses that they have and the odd-looking humpy shoulders. To my eye, though, they are handsome in the same way that many noted and noble people are—maybe not classically good-looking, but regal, like Henry David Thoreau or Abraham Lincoln. You can't help seeing the grace and dignified bearing when you look at them. And then when a moose moves through the forest, legs working like pistons, stepping over logs and rock walls, slipping through the brush, holding that massive head high, you know that you are seeing something special, even if it is just a quick look.

In 2005 I teamed up with the Massachusetts Division of Fisheries and Wildlife to initiate a study of moose in Massachusetts. It is natural to want to know something about what these big animals are doing in a state like this, and one good way to find out is to put on the telemetry collars that send out signals so that you can locate individual animals in their movement across the landscape. In recent years, the Global Positioning System (GPS) has given us the ability to locate ourselves on the earth in our planes and boats and cars, and even as we walk around, if we have a handheld GPS unit. Same is true for wildlife, if you can persuade them to let you put a collar on them. If you can, the collar will communicate with satellites—every one to two hours, twenty-four hours a day, in the case of our study on moose—and the satellites send the information back to the collar on earth, like wisdom from the heavens.

One day in midwinter I took to the field with two young guys, Dave Wattles and Ken Berger, wondering how long I would be able to keep up. We had already been out for several days, slowly driving along logging roads and hiking around, looking for sign, watching for animals. We peered out the side windows as we drove up a road somewhere in the heart of the Prescott Peninsula on the Quabbin watershed. When I turned to look forward I saw the huge hump of a thing looming over the crest of the road up ahead. We all said "Moose!" at once, and as we did, it turned and moved to the south, high-stepping over logs and brush as if they were nothing, with those white-stockinged legs propelling the massive body forward in a fluid movement. For a moose, it wasn't moving fast, but it covered the ground too swiftly for us ever to keep up.

By a year afterward, I had seen several moose. One day in midwinter I was standing behind a large boulder in the woods of north-central Massachusetts, waiting to see if the guys might push a moose past me close enough to allow a shot at it with the dart rifle. Up to that date we had gotten eight or nine of the GPS collars out, as good, or better, a result as I had hoped for when I saw my first Massachusetts moose a year before.

I was listening to the talk on the radio as Dave and Ken proceeded with the drive. They were seeing lots of sign and hearing movement out in front of them. It was a clear, cold day and the wind was up, bandying the branches about overhead and all around me. At a moment when I wasn't expecting it, I heard one footfall and the snapping of a single twig. I looked up the slope above me, and just as I did, a magnificent bull moose walked into my line of sight. He heard the radio and saw me and stood looking down at me. He hadn't shed his antlers yet. They were well balanced but not huge. I slowly reached for the radio and switched it off, my eyes never leaving his. I thought of lowering the dart rifle and trying for the left front shoulder, but I worried about the chances of the dart's deflecting and hitting him in the face. So I waited for him to turn, know-ing that he would continue up over the ridge. When he did, I would bring the gun to my shoulder and get off a shot at his rump. The safety was off. My finger hovered near the trigger guard. I was ready. We continued to stare at each other.

Then he turned and I lowered the gun. I got him in the scope and saw a dark, hairy mass moving in a line from right to left. I needed one second to focus, but I didn't get it. He disappeared behind a dense clump of young hemlock and was gone, leaving me with only a story and a set of tracks to follow down the other side of the ridge.

The realization that wildlife is truly a part of the suburbs has crept up behind us while we out were watering the lawn. Attracted by the smell of food and the scent of water, shelter from winter weather, safety from predation, or the combination of a variety of resources and factors that make suburbia inhabitable for some forms of wildlife, animals of all sorts have shown up underfoot and overhead, occupying the niches that the built environment holds for them. It is common knowledge now and reported daily in the newspapers, on television, in conversations among neighbors. We read the local police reports of black bears showing up at birdfeeders in the spring or the front-page article about the coyote appearing at the edge of the schoolyard. The moose wandering through a neighborhood is seen on the nightly news. Most suburbanites, and urbanites, are now well aware of the wildlife that may live in their neighborhood. These are the animals that have moved back into the area or maybe never left at all. And some of them, like moose and bears and coyotes, are big, are often unpredictable, and can be worrisome.

You don't need to have large animals like moose, bears, or coyotes in your backyard, though, to know that wildlife is around. No matter where you live, wild creatures of some sort will be living with you, often closer than you would like to think. Parasitologists say that if you lay any human being down on a large dark sheet and take away everything but the parasites, you will see a distinct outline of the human form—that's how pervasive parasites are in our bodies. In the same vein, the U.S. Department of Agriculture states that a certain level of insect parts and rodent hair and feces is acceptable in the nation's food supply.[1] Most people are aghast when they first hear this, and they may protest the incompetence of the federal government, but it would not matter if the USDA established a zero-tolerance policy for these animal parts and by-products in our food supply. No government program, no amount of scrutiny or monitoring, filtering, screening, or cleansing would keep all the wings, legs, antennae, down feathers, hairs, and turds out of our grains and produce, so common are pests in our food supply.

Biologists delight in repeating these facts, especially over lunch or dinner. The real point is that nature in all its forms—invertebrate or vertebrate, plant, fungi, bacteria, or virus—is integrated into the human world. That statement is really just another way—although perhaps a less poetic or appealing way—of saying that humans are a part of all nature, something that we know but tend to forget.

The truth is, nature finds a way to exist almost anywhere. Not all forms can survive in all places—grizzly bears or golden eagles or even wood turtles are not likely to flourish in suburbia—but some form of life can be found just about everywhere. For virtually every set of environmental conditions on earth, organisms exist that can exploit those conditions. Life is present in the very deepest parts of the oceans, the coldest reaches of the Arctic and Antarctic, the hottest deserts, and the most remote islands. In fact, the primitive prokaryotes known as archaea, which are thought to be among the earliest forms of terrestrial life, can thrive in conditions intolerable for most of earth's life forms.[2] Known collectively as extremophiles, these microbes can live in extremely high temperatures (in the case of hyperthermophiles) or extremely low ones (in the case of psychrophiles), in high pressure (barophiles), or acidic environments such as sulfur pools (acidophiles), or even in the tiny pores within rocks (endoliths). We may find them yet in the rocks or recesses of some other planet in our solar system or beyond. As long as the most basic necessities of life are available, some organisms will be able to survive, reproduce, and flourish. Now that we humans are a major ecological driving force on earth, we create conditions that will be favorable to some species but not to others. Thus, as sprawl claims the landscape, some species will be driven out and others will stay or find welcome. In many ways you cannot pick your neighbors, regardless of species—they establish residency if they like the neighborhood and the conditions are right. As a result, the list of species that could be called suburbophiles is relatively long.

As is true of insects and other invertebrates, so it is with larger animals. Numerous kinds of wildlife live among us and occupy the innermost niches in the biggest of cities. John Kieran, a devoted naturalist, describes in great detail in his classic *A Natural History of New York City* (1959) the myriad invertebrate, vertebrate, and plant species that live in and around New York City.[3] Starting, as he writes, "in a small way," with seaweed and mollusks, then progressing through fish and insects, amphibians, reptiles, plants, and mammals, and ending with birds (the only group to merit two full chapters), Kieran lists and describes the natural history and wildlife of his city, telling us not only what you can find and where, but which species you are not likely to find, and which species you once could find in the area but now cannot. Overall, his message is one of optimism and enthusiasm, perhaps born of a time before recognition of the true impact of sprawl and the human presence: "Let the population of the area increase and multiply as it may, let men build and pave to their heart's content, there will always be many kinds and untold numbers of wild things in the great city." Dr. Kieran was at least partly correct, although I would guess we would find less diversity there now than when he made his astute observations and kept his careful records half a century ago. Still, Kieran's life's work is a testament to the persistence of nature in New York and all other large cities of the world.

Different groups or species of wildlife will respond to human environments, both urban and suburban, in different ways: that is important to keep in mind. In considering an article that my colleague and friend Dick DeGraaf and I wrote on the ecology of suburban wildlife, the editor of the journal kept asking, Is suburbia bad or good for wildlife?[4] She wanted a definitive answer. Well, it can be either, depending on the circumstances and the species. Several species do very well in the most urban of areas throughout the world, and actually might not even be around (certainly not in the great numbers or distribution in which we find them) had it not been for their human partners' unwitting creation of a favorable environment for them. Many of these urban species are non-native, introduced, exotic species that are almost universally associated with people.[5] The European starling, the house sparrow, the house finch, the domestic pigeon or rock dove, the common mynah, the spotted dove, the house mouse, and the Norway rat are among the most synanthropic vertebrate species in the world.[6] They are the wild animals living in close proximity to or closely associated with humans—not exactly a list of species that motivates a bird-watcher or amateur naturalist, but they are what they are, and they are definitely well adapted to the many parts of the planet that we have changed.

Some native species are adapted to life in cities and towns. They may do just fine in exurban environments, but some aspects of town life suit them. In North America, robins, mockingbirds, chickadees, gray squirrels, cottontail rabbits, mallard ducks, and chipmunks can be counted as backyard or neighborhood wildlife. Raccoons, skunks, opossums, and white-tailed deer also inhabit cities and suburbs, though these animals are often not welcome, because they get into our garbage, eat our ornamental plants, burrow under our decks and sheds, and otherwise take advantage of the situation. We call these species pests when they cause us problems or become an annoyance.

A whole host of other species, however, do not do well with development. Many songbirds, large mammals, reptiles and amphibi-ans, fish, and other creatures—butterflies and moths and plants and fungi—struggle and decrease in number as human presence increases. Large carnivores are often the first to vanish in the face of human de-velopment of the landscape. The numbers of wolves, grizzly bears, and even bobcats start to dwindle as human population density grows.[7] Species that have specialized niches are also vulnerable. When you eliminate or degrade a specific type of habitat, and it is the only place where you find a certain species, that species will disappear from the area. Human presence and development of the environment is a com-plex and dynamic process. Not all wildlife species are affected in the same way, and even the same species may respond differently to vary-ing kinds of alterations.

In general, so much variation is present in nature, not only in the variety of species in the world but also in their relationships and func-tions (the subject of ecology), that biological scientists have estab-lished relatively few immutable laws or well-founded theories of the sort that exist in physics, chemistry, and astrophysics. Two of them are the cell theory (all living things are made up of cells) and the theory of evolution based on natural selection (species change over time on the basis of survival of the fittest). Another one might well be that biodiversity—which the scientist and naturalist E. O. Wilson saw as "the greatest wonder of this planet"—decreases as human population and development expand.[8] Some species will increase in the subur-ban landscape to the point of being labeled overabundant, but ev-erywhere fewer species, including all the vertebrate groups (fish, am-phibians, reptiles, mammals, and birds) will thrive in the landscapes of urban and suburban sprawl, in proportion to the level of develop-ment. When we examine the most heavily developed regions of the world, we see a trend toward reduced diversity and increased homoge-neity among species. The species that do exist in these human envi-ronments are often extremely abundant, but many other species are ei-ther missing or barely hanging on.

Among the many reasons for this diminution are the loss, alter-ation, and simplification of habitat. Fill in the wetlands and you will no longer have wetland-dependent amphibians; cut down or thin the woods and you will no longer have nesting birds that require interior woodlands. Increase the numbers of roads and traffic, and many animals will be crushed by cars, a factor that can have a dire effect on the viability of local populations.[9] Introduce marauding house cats, which are excellent hunters, and the population of small mammals and birds will suffer.

At the same time, some features of the human developed landscape form habitat for certain species—for example, lawns for starlings and robins, shade trees for squirrels, foundations of sheds and other buildings that can be used by skunks and opossums. Human environments can supply abundant cover, water, and food, and animals are constantly on the lookout for all three, especially food. If it is there—and our dumps, garbage cans, dumpsters, flower and vegetable gardens, lawns, and ornamental trees and shrubs provide great bounty—wildlife will find it. And these offer just the unintentional leavings of our society. When artificial feeding is added to the mix, whether in a form considered to be good or neutral, such as at bird feeders, or negative, such as in corncribs (for deer), in dog dishes (for coyotes, foxes, and bears), or through dumping of bread, popcorn, and the like on the ground (for ducks and gulls), plenty of food is available for the taking. Wild animals respond to abundant food with increased presence, improved survival, and enhanced reproduction. The formula almost always applies: more food means more animals.

Therefore, we should consider at least three types of species when thinking about suburban wildlife: (1) those which, being highly synanthropic and largely dependent on humankind for their wide distribution and local abundance, live pretty much only in human environments; (2) those which do poorly in human environments and whose populations are declining or nonexistent in areas of human development; and (3) those which can take advantage of almost any situation, whether rural, wild, or suburban. All three groups of species are part of the ecology of urban/suburban areas.

🐾 Winter came late that year, but when it did, it arrived cold and snowy. The female coyote is fully furred out now, looking two to three times her actual body size because of the thick underfur and long guard hairs. She is mostly gray and white, with blondish highlighting and edgings of black. There are rufous patches around her ears and face and on her lower legs. She trots across the snow, avoiding the deeper drifts when she can, wading when she has to. She takes to footpaths and deer trails more often than not, traveling through the woodlands in a quiet, fluid motion, like water over ice.

She has been wandering this way for several months, leaving a gently meandering line of footprints, a bit longer than they are wide, two inches by three inches, in the snow. The paired sets from the front and hind paws are about a foot or more apart when she is moving at a relaxed pace, a bit farther apart—fourteen to fifteen inches—when she is in more of a hurry. For the past few days her tracks have led back to the same spot, a deer carcass by the side of a state highway. The deer was hit almost a week ago and was thrown by the impact down into a ditch several feet from the road edge. Now it is hidden from motorists by the falling snow and the berm left by the town plows. The body lies broken and frozen, but the coyote was able to gnaw into the body cavity to get at the liver, lungs, and heart—the best parts—before having to share the remainder with the local ravens and crows. She came back and fed on the carcass for three days, gorging on frozen meat. A fox has also been around some, but he is wary of the coyote. A few quick pulls on the hindquarters afford him some small mouthfuls. He wants more but instinctively knows it is risky, so he takes what he can and moves on, mousing through the soft snow in a meadow some distance away.

Under most conditions it would take more than her hunting skills alone for the coyote to bring down an animal as large as a deer. When the day came for her to join a pack or form one of her own, they could all go out in a group of, say, three or four or more and attempt larger kills. Deep snow or the chance to chase a deer out onto the ice of a large lake would give the pack an advantage. The deer that would eventually fall to the coyotes would not necessarily be old or infirm. It could be relatively healthy but hampered by the snow and ice. Perhaps it would happen later in winter, when the cold and snow and the struggle to survive had it worn down a bit. At that point, a deer could be outmaneuvered by a small pack of skillful and resourceful hunters.[10]

For now, though, the carrion has been a good find for the female. It is helping her get through. Winter is a long season here. She eats her fill and retires to sleep some of it off. She spends a lot of time holed up in temporary dens. Nothing fancy—she may curl up in a shallow depression at the base of a stump, or lie tucked up under a narrow rock ledge that has kept some oak leaves dry, or rest in an abandoned shed, the only thing left standing of an old New England dirt farm. She weathers it all: the freezing temperatures, ice storms, deep snow, long, dark nights, and dimly lit days.

At some point, weeks later, she raises her head quickly from her day bed. Some new sound has all of a sudden claimed her attention. She focuses ahead and to the left, staring through the trees as if she can see the horizon. Her ears are perked forward, her eyes unblinking. She is not moving, but she is watching, listening, taking it in. The noise is all around her, but she focuses on the sound coming from straight ahead: it is the dripping of melting snow from the trees and the stirring sound of running water.

CHAPTER 6

The Suburban Jungle

🌿 A soft cooing drifts out of the arroyo like a cottonwood seed on an updraft. The morning is bright and clear, perfectly cool for a while, as the sun makes its way up in the sky. It will start to feel warmer by nine o'clock, and by ten unmistakably hot. By noon the sun takes over this territory and makes it its own, maintaining possession of it until day's end, when it sinks behind the sharp rise of distant mountains.

I am not far away in miles, but quite a distance away in landscape and lifestyle, from the urban jungle of Tucson, a city that has spread until it not only fills up the Tucson Basin but has begun a slow creep up the slopes of the surrounding mountains. Now I stand, some sixty or so miles to the south, in a place that has been called Buenos Aires, Good Air, for the past many decades. The straight line of the Mexican border lies within eyeshot. Multiple strands of barbed wire mark the dividing line between the two cultures that lie on either side. The peak of Baboquivari, the high point in the nearby Baboquivari Mountains, shines in the morning light like a monument to God. It is clear why the Tohono O'odham (Desert People) believe that their creator lives on that pinnacle. He sent them into the valleys to populate the earth and live among other members of creation in a desert named the Sonoran. Centuries ago it must have been a harsh existence in this land, marked by times of drought and starvation, and yet a beautiful one, graced by times of abundance. In those days life here meant an acceptance of both.

Mesquite trees dot the landscape, as if in reminiscence of an ancient and familiar landscape from a continent a world away, a savanna of dry heat and bunchgrasses, a home for early hominids, who bravely descended from the trees and wandered out onto more open land in search of new territory and food. We started that practice way back when and have never given it up, as we have wandered and spread and occupied. I wonder what our world would be like had we just stuck to the trees.

I drive along slowly and stop at the next place. I turn off the engine and step quietly out of the pickup. I stand listening and looking at the dryness but greenness of this land that is known for its contrasts. And then there it is again, the soft coo in the distance. A quiet call, not to me—I just happen to be there listening—but to the others of its kind, its conspecifics. The low tone and gentle cadence of the sound are deceptive: it beckons some down over the rolling swale of the bajada, but the call carries a meaning quite different for others, a notice to stay away from this piece of occupied ground.[1]

An hour and a half later and twelve kilometers down the two-track I listen again, but the calls have ended. The sun is well up, and I pull my hat down to keep the strength of it off my face and neck. There is a new silence to the day and the arroyos seem a bit empty as I get into the truck and drive away.

Saturday morning—I am about thirty feet up the biggest ladder I have, trying to put some semitransparent stain on the fascia of the highest gable of the house, when I see a small movement just under the bottom edge of the board. I immediately think it's wasps, because they are incredibly common under the eaves and along the edge of the roof, but this is something different. It is bigger, and it is up under the narrow gap at the bottom of the board. Whatever it is, it is sidling away from me, obviously hoping that it can get far enough away so that I can't reach it or bother it.

I get my bearings on the ladder, put the brush into the hanging bucket of stain, grab on with both hands, and lean slightly to the right, peering up under the fascia. I see now that it is a little bat, probably a little brown bat, that is only seeking diurnal refuge in a tight little space under the wood, just the way it would under the bark or in the crevice of a tree.

I have seen lots of bats using our house for a roost. Before I tore off the old back porch, at least three to four bats would emerge from the roof of the porch near the corner post each evening in the summer and swoop out over the yard. I found another small roost site up under the old board-and-batten siding when I was tearing that off. Another time, I opened the basement door and heard a light plop on the ground. Looking down, I saw that it was a tiny bat, still folded up and probably stunned from the fall, that had been trying to roost between the upper edge of the door and the frame. I scooped it up in my gloved hand and brought it over to the wood pile, where I carefully placed it in a crevice in the wood. It clicked and chattered at me until I walked away.

I don't mind the company of bats. I really like it, in fact. They are welcome to the crevices and cracks in my house. They are quiet and respectful tenants, and they pay for their keep by eating pounds of insects and entertaining us with their aerobatic exploits on clear summer evenings. Can anyone say that is not way better than anything on television? I guess I may even prefer them to human neighbors. I have put up a couple of bat roost boxes on nearby trees but they haven't had much use, the bats preferring the house. I'm fine with that, as well.[2]

I finish up the final coat of stain quickly, so as not to disturb the little bat any more than necessary, and descend the ladder. From the safety of the ground I look up but see no movement. Pretty sure the tiny tenant didn't leave, I yank the ladder off the gable end. I feel satisfied that the bat is okay, tucked in and resting peacefully.

Our houses are often habitat for many of the animals that live in our suburban world.[3] These creatures are not usually shy about moving in, nor do they waste any time getting there. I have to laugh when I think about the spiders that live everywhere in and around my home. I swear, as I was nailing down the final boards on the soffits on the new addition to our house, spiders were following along behind me, taking up their positions and spinning their webs under the eaves, then vibrating to the thump of the nail gun without seeming to mind the disturbance at all. When we began the addition, we ended up evicting an entire colony of ladybird beetles (ladybugs) as we tore off the old boards. A year later they were back, quite comfortable under the new siding. Mud wasps and paper wasps are busy up under the high eaves every summer, and I don't think the flying squirrels ever really left. I may have beaten the carpenter bees, because the new wood is all freshly stained and they don't seem to find that as attractive as the older, worn trim boards, but just the other day I noticed a perfectly round hole close to the spot where soffit meets fascia. And the mice— deer mice where we live—make full use of all of the facilities; I expect they always will.

Outside, around the foundation and in the surrounding rock walls, chipmunks rule the universe or at least act as if they do. All kinds of snakes (garter, ringneck, milk, brown) also like the rock walls. Gray squirrels and red squirrels cavort in the treetops and on the building roofs and basically take over the bird feeders throughout the winter, easily thwarting my half-hearted efforts at squirrel-proofing. Every so often we see a raccoon prowling about the shed and chicken coop, to the constant consternation of the chickens. She is obviously interested in what is inside but has so far been unable to gain access. We have lost some chickens to an assortment of predators, but Ki and I don't mind much. We do what we can to protect our birds, but every so often a coyote or fox or weasel or hawk will outmaneuver us and nab one. We hide our cavalier attitude from the ladies for fear of their irate disapproval, but trust me, these hens live a pretty charmed existence.

Don't get me wrong—it's not that I welcome all these animals into the house and outbuildings and don't try to keep them out, or at least at bay. Periodically I sweep away the spiders, bomb the wasps, evict the squirrels, and wage war against the mice. I am quick to patch holes, and we always keep the dog food and chicken feed in mouse-proof containers. We secure our garbage, including the compost bins, and we even freeze bones and scraps of meat until we are ready to make a run to the dump. We put our bird feeders out late in the fall and take them in early in the spring, to avoid attracting bears. You can do lots of things yourself to "critter-proof" your house, and you can hire professionals to come and eliminate any life form that may have moved in, including dust mites and mold. Check the Web. All it takes is the will and the money—pest management achieves new levels of customer satisfaction these days. Do realize, though, that there is a very good chance that whatever you evict will be back: the continuing ebb and flow of us-against-them is all part of nature's plan. You and your house fit into the scheme of things, no matter how close you come to attaining *This Old House* perfection.[4]

The truth is, every place is habitat for some kind of wild flora and fauna. On a scale larger than our individual houses and yards our neighborhoods, towns, cities, and entire metropolitan areas can and do support biological communities. In fact, we now acknowledge that suburban and urban environments are ecosystems, either in and of themselves or as part of larger regional ecosystems. Ecological functions, such as hydrologic cycles, energy flow, and plant and animal community dynamics, occur within urban and suburban areas. Communities of species live and interact with one another and with their environment, and such ecological phenomena as plant succession, symbiosis, mutualism, competition, and predator-prey interactions take place within human communities. It is true, however, that most of these ecosystem processes occur in altered states, by comparison with more natural environments. It is important not only to accept the idea that urban and suburban areas are ecosystems, but to appreciate some of the differences between these human-dominated environments and wilder tracts of land.[5]

For one thing, impervious surfaces are much more extensive in urban and suburban areas than in exurban or natural areas. Rooftops, driveways, parking lots, and streets keep water from penetrating into the ground. Instead, rainwater and snow melt that flow over these surfaces are usually collected in storm drains and sewer systems and carried away. The loss of this water alters the dynamics of the hydrologic system, by affecting evaporation, groundwater recharge, erosion, and runoff. Runoff also tends to collect and concentrate pollutants, such as gas, oil, salt, and other compounds, in the water.

The vast expanses of hard surfaces, especially of concrete and asphalt, also collect and store heat; our cities have become "heat islands." The sun's energy builds up in these rocklike substances. It is retained during the day and released only very slowly as the evening progresses. The effect is especially dramatic in the Southwest, in cities like Phoenix and Las Vegas where daily temperatures easily top 100 degrees Fahrenheit during the summer. The undeveloped desert shows wide swings in temperature during a twenty-four-hour period: the daily high can reach 110 degrees Fahrenheit during daylight hours, but then temperatures can drop into the 70s at night, a difference of some 30 to 40 degrees within just a few hours. This pattern is called radiational cooling. Cities do not typically show such extremes in temperature over a short span of time: rather, cities hold the heat. In addition, the cooling nighttime hours do not last long enough to release much of that heat, so some is retained for the next day, when the heat builds up

again. When Ki worked on desert pronghorn and lived in the tiny desert town of Ajo in southern Arizona, she and her co-workers would bake out in the desert heat during the day, but then we would sit on her front porch in the evening, enjoying the fresh, cool desert air and listening to the coyotes howl, while Phoenix still sweltered in the 90s. The heat island effect is most dramatic in the desert, but you can also feel it in more northern cities like Boston and Minneapolis. Escaping the summer heat of the city is one of the reasons wealthy people in Boston built country estates during the 1800s in places like Watertown, which eventually became sprawling suburbs.

Urbanization and suburbanization have perhaps a more subtle effect than changes to water and energy (heat) cycles. Although building, maintaining, and running a city or town is no doubt a complex business, ecologically these areas are less diverse and more simplified in structure and function than the natural environment. Forests, wetlands, streams, coral reefs, and even grasslands and tundra are complex in structure and composition, and it is this complexity that provides niches for a variety of species. The built environment simplifies all that, and thus it comes as no surprise that a homogenization of species and a decrease in biological diversity tend to occur in cities and towns, even though some species do indeed thrive there. Fewer species inhabit urban and suburban environments, but members of the species that are present are often extremely numerous.

Like the cities and towns themselves, the patches of habitat and vegetation that do exist within the built environment also tend to be simpler in both structure and species composition. The landscape is more groomed: grass is mowed, trees are thinned out and pruned, the understory and any brush are cleared away, and dead and dying standing and downed wood (snags and logs) are removed. We have very pleasant and comfortable parks and yards and cemeteries left, but we are missing the habitat components that provide a variety of niches for a broader array of organisms—such as the brushy undercover that offers nesting places for many species of songbirds and escape cover for rabbits and other small mammals.

Disturbances, both natural and man-made, can cause habitats to become fragmented, but on some level disturbances are a part of natural ecosystems. We have learned recently that the seemingly destructive forces of fire, flood, wind, and even insect outbreaks can play an important constructive role in many natural ecosystems. In fact, some environments, like ponderosa pine forests, are fire-dependent, and riparian corridors rely on big, periodic floods. Without those large-scale disturbances, things change. The problem comes in when human activities alter both the spatial and the temporal scale of these processes; that is, humans influence where the processes happen, how often they occur, and the size of the affected area. One classic example is Smokey the Bear: he "oversold" the value of preventing forest fires to such an extent that natural fire cycles that occurred in the past have been drastically disrupted. We have hindered fire in the West so assiduously that the absence of fire actually causes a build-up of fuel. When these tremendous stores of fuel eventually ignite, the results are often cataclysmic. Catastrophic wildfires destroy large amounts of property and take many lives.

In our human-dominated environments we do two things that affect disturbances to the natural order (beyond the massive alteration of the environment to begin with, that is). First, we deter large-scale periodic disturbances such as floods (the largest of which are often called hundred-year floods) and fires, because we cannot have those things happening in our built environment, obviously. Second, at the other end of the spectrum we introduce frequent small-scale disturbances, such as mowing, brush clearing, pruning, and leaf removal, that interfere with the structural diversification that promotes biodiversity. I am not saying that any of this is bad. In fact, most of it is necessary and desirable. But it is an example of another difference between the urban-suburban environment and more natural areas.

One of the most talked-about threats to conservation is habitat fragmentation, and in cities and towns fragmentation can be pervasive and extreme. Here vegetation exists as patches, such as parks, yards, golf courses, and even median strips and vacant lots. These patches are not uncommon, but they are not often connected. Rather, they exist as separate entities, cut off from one another by roads, buildings, parking lots, and other features of the built environment. The islandlike patches in urban-suburban areas vary in composition and size and are set in a surrounding matrix of developed land. As development spreads, these patches become smaller and more isolated from one another. Fewer and fewer species can deal with this kind of habitat fragmentation, and so the diversity of species declines. Habitat fragmentation is a major concern for wildlife biologists, conservation biologists, and landscape ecologists throughout most of the world, and a wealth of information has been published on the topic, starting with the theory of island biogeography.[6]

Of the species that do tend to do well in urban and suburban environments, many are non-native species.[7] Also called exotics, because they originated in other regions of the world, or invasives, because they infiltrate and often aggressively colonize new territory, these species can outcompete the native fauna and flora. Several of the most infamous of exotic species gained their notoriety because they spread so rapidly and dominate areas, often to the point of becoming monocultures. Among the plant species known for their invasiveness we could mention purple loosestrife, tamarisk, and Japanese knotweed, but there are also many species of invertebrates, such as zebra mussels and a host of insect pests, and several species of vertebrates, such as starlings and house sparrows, whose local abundance can be significant. Often you do not find these species far from developed epicenters, and in fact the spread and proliferation of non-native species can be correlated with the spread and proliferation of human development. We encourage and subsidize exotics either knowingly, by planting or releasing organisms, or unknowingly, as happens when foreign beetle larvae enter the country in wood products, or when exotic mussels attach themselves in their early life stages to the hulls of ships and travel to foreign ports. The collection of organisms that results from such rapid dispersal is very different from the selection that was found there originally—that is, the community of native plants and animals. Ecologists have described the new assemblage, with its mix of some native species and many new, alien, exotic species, as a recombinant biological community.[8] The alteration of species composition in urban and suburban environments also brings about a shift in trophic relationships and food web dynamics, along with increases in and stabilization of certain species because of resource subsidies, and other changes in biological community dynamics because of the complex relationships, processes, and forms of feedback that exist between human and animal populations living in close proximity to one another.[9] In other words, as we alter the landscape through our activities, we affect the relationships, interactions, and processes of ecology, creating conditions that favor some species but hinder others. In a sense, the cities of the world are one giant experiment, unprecedented in scope and scale. Our knowledge of ecology can help us predict some of the consequences of urbanization, and our ability to adjust our lifestyles and plan the cities of the future can direct some of the outcomes. For the most part, though, we must wait to see what we have set in motion during these past several decades in the age of urban living.

Species that do inhabit towns and cities encounter new challenges. Heavy traffic, accidents due to other causes (such as collisions with windows), toxins, animal control through trapping and poisoning, and even occasional marauding bands of children pose dangers that are not unique to urban and suburban areas but are present in greater profusion. Predation is also a major source of mortality for many urban and suburban animals. Predation is an event that is not often witnessed by people. Once or twice I have seen Cooper's hawks blaze through yards and nail songbirds by snatching them off bird feeders. In fact, urban environments can foster higher concentrations of some raptor species than exurban areas do because of the greater prevalence of available prey and nesting sites.[10] To give another example, a graduate student of mine saw a weasel disappear near the foundation of her house one day, and then moments later saw a bunch of flying squirrels bail out of the attic. Those rarely observed events are pretty exciting. Yet it is our domestic animals—I'm speaking, of course, about dogs and cats—that may kill the most significant number of wild animals. Dogs, especially when they form packs, are pretty proficient at running down prey. Often the pursuit takes the form of harassment: giving chase and running animals up trees or into the ground, occasionally catching some and killing them. Nothing, however, compares with cats. Cats may be the most efficient predators on the planet, and the domestic cat has filled a niche in the human environment so perfectly that no other animal even comes close.

Cats are the ideal urban predator. They have everything going for them: stealth, skill, intelligence, and even good looks and an astounding amount of charisma. The last two may not seem like very objective thinking coming from a biologist, but I believe they are the traits that allow cats to be so incredibly successful in our human-dominated world.

On a recent trip to Saint John in the Caribbean, Ki and I were impressed with (and concerned about) the numbers of cats inhabiting the island. They were everywhere that people were. One morning as we sat and drank coffee under the canopy of gumbo-limbo and black mampoo trees, I watched two black cats, perfectly matched, make their way down a hillside by moving from tree limb to tree limb. They hopped with easy grace from the trees onto the roof of the coffee shack, and from there down onto a railing. They walked along that, one following the tail of the other, past the group of people sitting at tables. Everyone watched the pair go by, and several people remarked on how beautiful those cats were. They were probably on a hunt for something, because predators like cats almost always are; countless numbers of birds and reptiles fall prey to domestic cats every year. Yet not many people mind that, at least certainly not to the point where they would want cats removed or destroyed. Mongooses live on the island, as well, but they move like weasels and have faces like rats, so people are not as enamored of mongooses. But cats are pretty, and we like pretty.

Later that evening we sat down to supper at an outdoor restaurant, where the cats were out doing their thing, wandering among the tables, working the crowd. They would sit on the ground next to people but look away, feigning lack of interest—an attitude that none of us can resist. I have to admit, I even had a favorite: a calico-colored female that I called Mustard because she had a blotch of yellow on her chin. She seemed to know just when to be aloof and when to rub up against my leg. The cats pretty much commanded the attention and admiration of everyone. It's more or less hopeless for conservationists who like little native birds, admire lizards, and root for all manner of small mammals—the native fauna will be hit hard, because felines rule. Given their style and good looks, not to mention their skills and abilities, cats are here to stay; and we are unlikely to do much to control their numbers or to keep them from roaming free, despite the good efforts of conservation groups that advocate for keeping them indoors.

Urban and suburban environments are indeed ecosystems that have many unique and interesting features. Chief among these are lawns. In an early study of the lawn as ecosystem, the ecologist John Falk described lawns as "grasslands of uniform height and of constant species makeup," an ecologist's way of saying that we keep them short and favor a few species, like bluestem, over others, such as crabgrass and dandelions.[11] Falk went on to describe the animal life resident in his twelve-hundred-square-foot lawn in Contra Costa County, California, that formed the object of his study. The enormous variety of living things that make their home in lawns is a testament more to the power of species to thrive in all kinds of environments than to the ability of lawns themselves to foster biodiversity. The long list of animal occupants includes aphids, leafhoppers, midges, mites, thrips, pill bugs and sow bugs, springtails, earwigs, snails and other mollusks, all manner of flies, ants, and spiders, rove beetles, and parasitoid wasps. His list of the birds that frequent lawns included scrub jays, Brewer's and red-winged blackbirds, starlings, and house sparrows. In the East you could add robins and flickers. Squirrels, skunks, voles, moles, and deer mice are mammals that make use of lawns. Canada geese are particularly attracted to lawns and spend a great deal of their time grazing on the green growth and leaving behind lots of droppings.[12]

According to some authorities, we have between 25 million and 40 million acres of turf in the United States.[13] That is twice as much acreage as we have planted to cotton, and three times that planted to corn. Home lawns, numbering some 58 million, constitute the most common form. We also have 700,000 athletic fields and more than 16,000 golf course facilities. And who counts the median strips and grassy borders and little plots of grass that exist everywhere else? During the period from 1982 to 1997, the area covered by lawns grew by over 380,000 acres per year. According to one authority, lawn grass could be the largest irrigated crop in the United States, if we go by land coverage. And according to one estimate, to keep all that grass green requires the equivalent of two hundred gallons of fresh water per person per day in this country. The water bill no doubt makes up a large portion of the $40 billion Americans spend on lawn care each year.[14]

Of the fifty or so species of turf that make up lawns, few are native to the region where they are planted. The energy input required to maintain them is also great—not only of water but of fertilizer, weed killer, pesticides, and gas and oil for mowing, weed whacking, edging, leaf blowing, and so on. Lawn advocates are quick to point out the benefits of lawns, however.[15] In fact, even the U.S. Congress noted the benefits of grass (and other vegetation) in its Farm Bill of 1990, stating, "Low growing dense perennial turfgrass sod in urban areas and communities can aid in reducing carbon dioxide emissions, mitigating the heat island effect, and reducing energy consumption, thus contributing to efforts to reduce global warming trends."[16] The new emphasis on organic lawn care promises to curtail the harmful effects of pesticide and fertilizer runoff. So much is relative: in my hometown of Watertown, where parking spaces for cars have displaced the old front yards, I would far prefer to see more lawn and less asphalt.

Nonetheless, I have a healthy irreverence for lawns. It's not that I don't like them. We have lawn around our house, and I mow it during the summer with our little rechargeable mower. (It's great: no gas, no oil, no tune-ups, no winterizing, and it is pretty quiet and starts every time with a squeeze of the handle.) I have to admit that the yard does look nice when it is freshly manicured, and the dogs and chickens love it. We don't water it or fertilize it, and the weeds, mosses, and some very pretty little flowers—bluets I think—take over in patches (fine with me). Thus it is lawn (if you can call it that) by virtue of survival of the fittest, which has been my gardening approach ever since my days in Tucson, where it is the heat and dryness that dictate which things live and which die. Around here in southern New England we usually have enough summer rain to keep the grass growing through at least the first two-thirds of the season, so mow you must. Regardless of the necessity, mowing seems an odd way to spend a good part of a summer evening or weekend.

It occurs to me that we humans spend way too much time moving biomass around—grass in the summer, leaves in the fall—not to mention snow all winter long. Life is too short. So I leave the clippings in the freshly mowed backyard, and come fall I'll let the wind blow the leaves back into the woods. Right now it is time to pull the lawn chairs onto the grass and kick back, have a beer with my wife, talk about the day, watch the dogs wrestle and the chickens scratch and fuss, and admire the dandelions. What better way to spend a fine spring evening in late April (which by the way is National Lawn Care Month, in case you didn't know)?[17]

🐾 The female has reached the end of her second winter and consequently is at the age when many of her kind meet their end. She is in pretty good shape, however. She has been finding enough food, has avoided traffic so far, and has made it through a couple of hunting seasons. She could live another three to four years or more. Although coyotes have been known to live up to fifteen years in captivity, it is not likely she will live to anywhere near that age. Ten years would be a pretty ripe old age for most wild and free-ranging coyotes.

Death can find a coyote in many ways. For most of their history timber wolves were a major cause of mortality among coyotes. Wolves can outrun and outmaneuver coyotes, and when they catch them, they invariably kill them. Coyotes never need to be told this twice, and so they mostly avoid the areas where wolf packs have established their territories. That precaution, most biologists believe, kept coyotes out of eastern North America; but when we humans succeeded in our campaign against the wolf, we opened up the country to coyotes, and they stepped in.

Despite the possibility of mating with a domestic dog, the coyote avoids dogs wherever and whenever she can. Dogs have been known to kill coyotes. The female instinctively moves away from the signs and smells of dogs. She will take risks from time to time and enter yards in search of food where dogs live, but her careful reconnaissance keeps her apprised of the size and potential threat of the local dogs and the habits of their owners—for example, whether they keep their pets in a kennel or on a lead or locked up in the house at night. It is in her best interests to know these things, and being a careful hunter with a couple of years' experience, she keeps track of the situation in the area she roams. The risk comes when she ventures into new and unknown territory.

Human beings can cause the greatest number of deaths among coyotes. Hunting, animal damage control, and run-ins with automobiles are the most common causes of death across the coyotes' range. But the same has become true for many forms of wildlife. We humans dominate the world in many ways, and we are often intentionally or unintentionally the leading cause of death among animals. In several studies, human-induced mortality accounted for more than 90 percent of total mortalities in coyote populations.

Starvation can occur at any time, and it does. So many of the female's waking hours are spent searching for food that anyone who could follow her schedule would realize that her life is a race to keep malnutrition at bay. It seems amazing that this could be the case for a species whose diet is so eclectic. Diseases like mange and parvovirus also fell coyotes. We don't often think of accidents affecting wild animals, except of course for motor vehicle accidents, but in the rough-and-tumble lifestyle that most animals live out in the untamed world, accidents such as falls and other injuries do occur. It is tough to make it as a predator if you have a serious injury, but it is also amazing what individual animals can overcome.

A lot of things out there can spell the end of a coyote's life. Every study ever done on the subject marks and tallies the ways in which the research subjects die, but a final category invariably accounts for a large percentage of total mortality: "unknown." Coyotes' cause of death often remains undiscovered, and most coyotes pass from this life in the way that they lived it, far from the prying eyes of their human observers.[18]

CHAPTER 7

A Trilogy of Tolerable Nuisances, Part 1

Traffic

It is early July in the northern Great Basin Desert. I am out in my pickup, just as the sun disappears behind a ridge of faraway mountains. As the day fades, so does the intense summer heat. In the distance I can see the lights from a few vehicles as they travel the single highway, which runs like a dark black band across the ancient lava rocks and sandy soil of the desert floor, north to Burns or south to the Nevada border. The traffic is light, as it always is in this remote corner of Oregon, and so far away that the movement of the few vehicles is marked only by the steady glare of their headlights. The sound of the car engines is swallowed up by the desert and dissipated into the atmosphere before it reaches me. I sit in relative silence, waiting for the remnants of daylight to follow the sun down below the horizon.

As it begins to grow dark and cool, I hear scurrying amid the sagebrush and greasewood, as kangaroo rats, pocket mice, and other small rodents begin their nightly forays to look for food. From within a nearby hole, sand and gravel slide downward in small trickles as an animal emerges from its den. A sleek muzzle bordered on both sides by dark stripes, a pair of large eyes, and two oversized ears appear above the surface of the ground and test the wind and the sights and sounds of early evening. The expressive face is followed by a body with grayish back and yellowish flanks, and finally a long, bushy tail that ends in a black tip and almost matches the body in length. A kit fox has just stepped out into the desert world. The tiny fox—only about five or six pounds in weight and about the size of a jackrabbit—moves away from its den site, making a break across a stretch of open ground before slipping quietly into the hip-high brush. It travels off to the south and west.

I spent a year searching for these little foxes in the high desert of southeastern Oregon.[1] I hiked during the day to look for tracks and scats, traveled down roads and ran transects through sagebrush, across sand flats, and over dunes. At night I was out from sundown to sunrise, broadcasting the shrill distress calls of rabbits and birds over a small megaphone to attract predators (like kit foxes), and using a powerful spotlight equipped with a red filter to see what might come in. The light would reflect off the animals' eyes and make them shine. It was as if the creatures had bright lights of their own inside their heads. I could see the glowing sets of eyes of coyotes as they came loping in toward the calls, long before I could make out their form in the filtered light. Mule deer would stand at attention and face the sound before fleeing. Badgers would sit upright at the mouth of their holes. Cows would look up for a moment, the light from their eyes shining back dimly, before lowering their heads again.

Some folks thought that kit foxes, after decades and probably centuries of occupying this corner of Oregon, had disappeared, for who knows what reason?—too many coyotes, overgrazing, too-harsh winters, or just the fact that they were at the northern end of their range and therefore prone to vanish and reappear, apparently at random. In the weeks I was out looking, I found what I thought might be kit fox tracks, but saw nothing more. Then one night, just past midnight and not far north of the Nevada border, I saw my first lone kit fox. I caught another one in my spotlight a few nights later, and then, best of all, a pair came right into the beam of my light in quick response to the predator call. After that, I began to see a few more animals and to find tracks on a more regular basis. It was clear that the nocturnal life of the high desert valleys, below the silhouetted form of Steens fault block and in the starlit shadows of the Trout Creek Mountains, still included kit foxes.

Seeing that pair bound across the sand to stand in my spotlight, side by side, ears up, was a good if brief moment in the otherwise quiet desert. They stood together for a minute, looking curious but twitching with impatience, as moonlight washed over the valley and cast an unearthly silver glow on the sagebrush. I stared down the beam of the beacon for as long as I could, until, with what seemed a blink, the shine of their eyes disappeared and they were gone.

I think about that pair of foxes as I make my way over the deserted dirt track and back to the highway. Dawn has just spread its light over the desert as I reach the pavement. There is no traffic, save for one car that comes seemingly out of nowhere, forcing me to wait a minute while it cruises past, before I roll onto the blacktop and head back home. 🐾

In a café in Tucson on a warm summer morning, I slide into a booth by the window, coffee in one hand, a copy of the *Arizona Republic* in the other. I sip my coffee—the kind New Englanders would call a regular coffee, nothing fancy, just hot coffee with cream and sugar—and peel back the pages of the newspaper. I come to a full-page ad for real estate and new homes that goes something like this: "Now you can have that six-car garage you've always wanted."

I laugh loudly enough to cause heads to turn. I think it's a joke. It isn't. A well-known developer in the Phoenix area is offering prospective buyers lots of options with the model homes that have just become available in his latest development, and among the extras is a garage that could house up to six vehicles. My amusement fades as quickly as it came. This is serious business—as serious as Americans are about their automobiles.

My first car was a beauty: a 1965 Pontiac Lemans two-door convertible with a blue body and a faded white roof that cost me $350 in 1977. It had a big V-8 engine: all power, no pollution control equipment. I bought it from an old lady who, I joked, drove it only to church on Sundays but must have hit every parked car along the way, because the passenger side was completely dented, from the tip of the front fender to the taillight on the rear panel. But the door worked, and I pounded out the dents as best I could. With a new set of tires and a refurbished white ragtop, it looked pretty good.

I loved driving that car. It had low-slung front bucket seats, a center shift console, and a blue vinyl interior. With the roof down it looked like a big blue boat, and it cruised like an ocean liner. I spent the last year of college working on it and driving it from UMass Amherst to the Quabbin Reservoir in central Massachusetts, where I would hike in the woods and take pictures of wildlife. That car carried me halfway across the country to graduate school in Madison, Wisconsin, in 1978. Soon after that, it went into decline and I couldn't afford the maintenance and repairs, so I sold it to a guy in northern Wisconsin who eventually totaled it just outside Green Bay.

I wish I still had that car. Now I would have the money to fix it up, maybe get the body repaired professionally, and, not being one to disregard a good cliché (whether in writing or in life), buy a pair of fuzzy dice for the mirror. I'm on my third vehicle now—a pickup truck that I've had for over fifteen years and plan on keeping for another five, if time and rust don't take it. I like it, too. I have to admit, when I am in the mood for driving and I am cruising on some rural highway with the radio tuned to a good country-western station, I feel great. There are times when I just love driving, and there are times when that vehicle is the best thing I own, largely because of what it represents: mobility and freedom and independence. I can go when and where I want to go—my own schedule . . . nobody's business. I'd be lying if I said I didn't like that.

I'm not alone. After 1969, the number of automobiles in the United States grew twice as fast as the number of people who drove them, until in 2003, when the number of cars actually outnumbered the number of drivers for the first time in our history.[2] Automobiles dominate the American scene, and the roads we drive on and the places we park dominate the scenery. The Germans may have perfected engineering, the Italians style, the Japanese reliability, and the Mexicans longevity in the automobile, but it is the Americans who have made the car part of the family. In my hometown, those fence line–to–fence line garden spots that made up almost every yard when I was a kid have given way to asphalted parking spaces for the family's third and fourth cars. Per capita vehicle ownership in the United States is the highest in the world, at close to 800 cars for every thousand people. That is almost one car for every man, woman, and child in the country. Western Europe is not too far behind, with about 550 cars per thousand people. Compare that figure to somewhere around 200 cars per thousand people in eastern Europe and the former Soviet Union, 150 in Central and South America, and 40 in China and developing Asia.[3] What will oil consumption and air pollution be like as those nations strive for a U.S. standard of car ownership?

With cars, of course, come traffic jams and gridlock—a terrible way to spend two to three hours of every day, but many of us do it. We complain about the congestion, but apparently it doesn't bother us enough to make us do anything about it, like design more user-friendly mass transportation. It is, as the author John Mitchell put it, a "tolerable nuisance" of suburban life.[4] We have forgotten—or maybe we never really knew—what life was like before traffic, and so the slow daily commute is just something we accept. Suburban development involves a lot of tolerable nuisances, of which traffic is only one of the more obvious.

Roadways in North America occupy some five million miles, to service an estimated 250 million vehicles. Our road system is the largest human artifact on earth, and Dr. Richard Forman, a professor of landscape ecology at Harvard University, has described it as an enormous net spread over the land. Roads are a prime example of the never-ending dichotomies of our modern life in the natural world. Fourteen coauthors, led by Dr. Forman, state it eloquently in the preface to their landmark book, *Road Ecology:*

> These two giants, the land and the net, lie intertwined in an uneasy embrace. The road system ties the land together for us yet slices nature into pieces. Natural processes degrade and disrupt roads and vehicles, requiring continuous maintenance and repair of the rigid network. Conversely, the road system degrades and disrupts natural patterns and processes, requiring management and mitigation for nature. Both effects—nature degrading roads and roads degrading nature—are costly to society.[5]

The road system, which we consider so central to our personal freedom, social mobility, and economic success, lies at the heart of our problems with sprawl and loss of open space. Roads carry us from place to place, notably from home to work, but also to grocery stores, shopping malls, hospitals, recreation sites, and the homes of friends—basically everywhere. I have always been amazed at the concept of taking five to six steps from my front door to my truck in Massachusetts, driving for days across the country, and then having to take only five to six steps from my truck to the front door of a friend's house in Oregon. Except for stops for gas and food, to catch some sleep and take a whiz, I can travel three thousand miles and at the same time make a journey of only a dozen steps. Roads connect us and all the things we do and the people we know the way nerves connect all the parts of our bodies to our brains. The old farmer was wrong: you *can* get there from here.[6]

In addition to enabling us to complete the familiar rounds of daily life—to go to the dentist's office, the hardware store, the fast-food restaurant—roads transport us to otherwise relatively remote areas. The rural gravel and dirt roads in northern Maine are more numerous than the paved and improved roads in southern Maine.[7] The road system within the national forests comprises almost as many roads (about 380,000 miles) as does the nation's interstate highway system (about 400,000 miles).[8] Roads get people and their all-terrain vehicles (ATVs), snowmobiles, motorboats, kids, dogs, radios, DVD players, barbecue equipment, cookware, lawn chairs, and fishing poles to most corners of the country.[9]

When new roads go in, new homes can be built, so roads and suburban development go hand in hand. The road is really the first physical step in the process that leads to sprawl. Accessibility is the key. Oftentimes, especially here in Western Massachusetts, dirt or gravel roads are built and maintained for years without attracting much apparent activity to the surrounding area. They lull you into a sense of tranquility and complacency. I often take the dirt roads to work, not so much as shortcuts, but because I can drive through woods and by fields and along old stone walls—the stuff I love about New England. And even though there is no traffic to speak of on my usual way to work, there is even less along the dirt roads. But then one day something changes: someone dies and leaves an heir a bunch of property, or a builder is out looking for new ground, and houses begin to spring up like mushrooms after a summer rain: vinyl-clad, roofed with architectural-style shingles, with tilt-to-wash windows and front doors with beveled-glass. If we somehow limited road building, suburban development would probably never reach the level of sprawl.

In the United States, roads and roadsides cover about 1 percent of the land, an area the size of Indiana.[10] That in and of itself is huge, representing an outright removal of wildlife habitat from the landscape (by virtue of the road itself, whether dirt, gravel, or paved) or an alteration of that habitat (by virtue of the roadside zone, which is mowed and subjected to gas, oil, and salt runoff). This concept has been dubbed the road-effect zone, a term indicating that the impact roads have on terrestrial and aquatic habitats and on wildlife populations reaches beyond the edge of the pavement.[11] The influence of the road extends more than three hundred feet on either side, for most ecological factors, such as the effects the road zone can have on amphibian populations and the assistance they give to the invasion and dispersal of exotic plants. The area of influence extends to more than half a mile in other cases; for example, many grassland birds avoid areas for half a mile on either side of a road. By contrast, the road zone could form a travel corridor for the southward dispersal of moose from Maine and New Hampshire into Massachusetts. Thus, in effect a road is not just the blacktop or gravel strip you see and drive on. A road encompasses the modified areas running along it on either side and the traffic that hums along it and the salt and chemical residues that spread out onto the land and into the water. The take-home message: roads affect natural processes and animal populations in many different ways.

The first-felt effect of roads on nature is mortality directly from road construction. As researchers Stephen Trombulak and Christopher Frissell state simply and succinctly in an article in *Conservation Biology:* "Road construction kills any sessile or slow-moving organism in the path of the road."[12]

In other words, a plant, a soil invertebrate, or a toad or salamander or snake in the wrong place at the wrong time is a goner. Perhaps more important, road building consumes land and takes a toll on both terrestrial and aquatic habitats. Again, Trombulak and Frissell, basing their assessment on U.S. Department of Transportation figures, tell us, "The 13,107,812 km [8,144,801 miles] of road lanes of all types in the conterminous United States, with an average width of 3.65 m [twelve feet] per lane, have destroyed at least 4,784,351 ha [11,822,370 acres] of land and water bodies that formerly supported plants, animals, and other organisms."

This estimate applies to the pavement or gravel itself and so involves a bit less land than the Indiana-sized area that includes roads and roadsides. Still, we are talking about an area the size of Vermont and New Hampshire combined. Either way, it is a lot of real estate.

Once the road is constructed, it continues to affect conditions in the physical environment on and around it, especially when it comes to water. Roads disrupt and alter flow and runoff patterns. The hard-packed, impermeable surfaces of roadways do not allow water to be absorbed into the ground. Consequently, soil moisture content is different around roads than away from roads, runoff is increased, and sedimentation deposition changes. That hard surface also contributes to the heat island effect.[13] Most roads, especially those covered with black asphalt, quickly build up heat and retain it much longer than do surfaces covered with vegetation.

Unpaved roads become highly compacted; then, during dry times, traffic sends dust into the air, and it spreads a long way. Dust on plants can affect photosynthesis, respiration, and transpiration, the processes that keep them alive and healthy. Apparently mosses and lichens are particularly susceptible to a burden of dust.[14]

Road maintenance and vehicle use add certain chemicals to the surrounding environment as well. Trombulak and Frissell in their article mention five general types of chemicals: heavy metals from gasoline, particularly lead, and from the salt used for de-icing; salt, which not only beats up the undercarriages of our cars but can be harsh on roadside vegetation and especially aquatic communities; organic pollutants; ozone from vehicles; and nutrients.

Roads, at least unpaved and little-used dirt roads that run through places like our national forests, can also be of some use to wildlife. When I worked in the North Cascades of Washington, I noticed that in wintertime coyotes got farther up the mountains on groomed snowmobile trails than they might have otherwise because of the deep snow. The U.S. Forest Service ran a grooming machine up and down some of its roads to make the conditions better for snowmobilers, and the coyotes took advantage of the packed snow and used the roads as travel lanes. A groomer-operator told me that he would often see lynx on the roads too, as he descended the mountains at the end of his run in the evening. I have seen deer, foxes, and other wildlife following roads through the woods, and the northern goshawk, a large forest raptor, will use logging roads (skid trails) as flight lanes to and from its nest. Along the coast, skunks follow human trails through the dune grasses to get to the beach where they will look for food at night. In general, wildlife will follow the path of least resistance, just as people do; and in heavy vegetation or rocky terrain, that is often some kind of trail or road.

Roads can assist a host of other species, too, but they may be ones we wouldn't care to help. Exotic species often spread via roads. Thoroughfares aid the process in three ways. The first is that road building and other disturbances create conditions that are favorable for many weedy plants. In a sense, road building sets back succession, often to bare soil, to create an environment where weedy exotics thrive. The second way that roads assist exotics is by stressing or removing native species and thus, for the invaders, reducing competition. And the third way that roads help in the spread of exotics is by increasing their ease of movement, often with our assistance.

As we travel, or as other animals use roads as corridors, we often carry plant seeds with us and thus distribute them along the way. Usually the spread of invasives is abetted unwittingly. At other times, however, it is a planned event. I met a rancher in Mexico who raised an exotic grass called buffelgrass. He had a barn full of the fluffy, featherlike seeds, including hundreds of bags of them ready for shipment to other parts of Mexico and Central and South America for use in soil stabilization along roads. It was a conservation biologist's nightmare: the wholesale export of an exotic invasive grass to large parts of the Western hemisphere.

The access that roads provide not only helps some invasive species of plants and animals but provides access for the species for which they are intended . . . us. This is not a bad thing: roads bring large numbers of people to national parks and forests and wildlife refuges, so that everyone can see and enjoy and appreciate nature. The enjoyment is crucial if we are to build the public support we need to protect these areas. But the very action of bringing people in can be detrimental to nature as well, for we often bring our unique forms of disturbance to the scene.

The most obvious connection between wildlife and roads is mortality from collisions with, or crushing by, automobiles—roadkill. Virtually every species is susceptible to being killed by cars and trucks on roads. We are perhaps more familiar with death on the roads of large- to medium-sized animals like deer, raccoons, porcupines, opossums, and squirrels. We become acutely aware of roadkill hazards in places like New England, Alaska, and much of Canada, where moose live. Moose are huge, they are often most active at dawn and dusk, and they seem to be built to maximize damage to the average sedan. I have had them walk out in front of me on roads in Maine; the bumper of the car I was driving was just above the level of their ankles, so if I hit one it would be at the low end of its legs, and the impact would send that massive body into my upper hood and windshield. Drivers who walk away from such an accident are lucky. The end result is usually at the very least a totaled vehicle and a dead moose. Hundreds of vehicle-moose collisions take place annually in places like Maine and Alaska, resulting in dozens of dead moose and a few dead people every year.[15]

Roadkill is especially common at night, when many animals are out roaming around and can be blinded by headlights (literally, the "deer-in-the-headlights" syndrome). Lots of animals get killed on roads during the day too, though. Chipmunks and squirrels have developed a predator avoidance behavior that relies on rapid changes in velocity and sudden reversals of direction. It works well against hawks and foxes, often not so well against station wagons and SUVs.

Many animals are just not equipped to deal with this relatively new source of mortality. Cars do not behave the way most predators do, and the conditions on and along roads and the way we travel compound the difficulty. Speed certainly kills—not only humans, but also wildlife. For some people all of the time, and for most of us some of the time, going forty to fifty miles per hour in a thirty-mile-per-hour zone through a suburban neighborhood is the norm. At those speeds, drivers have no time to respond to wildlife (not to mention children), and animals that wander onto the asphalt have little chance. Add to that our propensity to tailgate, which forces the lead driver to go faster and draws his or her attention away from the road ahead, and the result is often flattened fauna. Massachusetts road crews (not to mention scavengers like crows and coyotes) are incredibly efficient at cleaning up the mess, however. My casual observations on the way to and from work indicate that it usually takes only one to two days for someone to find and remove a dead animal from a road. That's good, I guess; we wouldn't want to offend sensibilities by making people view the carnage as they drive.

Granted, most people would undoubtedly rather not hit animals. Still, I have been amazed at the behavior of some drivers. Recently, while traveling on Route 2 in central Massachusetts, I spotted a small flock of eight to ten Canada geese on the highway. They must have been attracted to the grass on the side of the road and had wandered into the right-hand lane, where I was driving. I had a line of cars passing me on my left, so naturally I slowed (to about forty to forty-five miles per hour; the speed limit was fifty-five) to allow the geese time to get back onto the shoulder. A woman behind me became extremely incensed that I had slowed down to such a speed. As she pulled out to pass, nearly clipping my bumper, she must have seen the geese on the road ahead. Nevertheless, she was so beside herself at having to slow down that she flew by staring at me, her mouth going and her hand gesticulating wildly. To her credit, she mouthed no swear words and made no obscene gestures, as far as I could tell, but she was incredibly upset.

A few months later, in late summer, I was heading back home up Route 202 North along the Quabbin Reservoir when I saw an adult bobcat attempting to cross the road. The reason for her caution became evident as she made her way onto the pavement—she had two half-grown kittens in tow. I stopped for her, and she passed right in front of me. I could see the kittens making false starts to follow their mom, but the blacktop and the openness of the road seemed to confuse and scare them. A guy in a sports car was coming down the other lane, so I put on my flashers, started flashing my headlights, and put up my hand to get him to stop or at least slow down. He did neither. Of course, just then the kittens made a break for it. I know he saw them, because I detected the look of recognition on his face. He may have lifted his foot off the gas for a moment, but if he did slow down, it was barely perceptible. The little cats darted out and, miraculously, made it across just under his tires. He gunned it past us all, obviously irritated at what must have been a three-second delay in his travel time. I gave him my most withering and disapproving look, which he of course completely ignored as he zoomed off.

Animals often need to cross roads because of their daily wanderings in search of food and other resources, or when they disperse to new territories. This is especially true of young animals at certain times of year. Our work with beavers in Massachusetts has shown that young animals, two to three years of age (subadults, biologists call them—that is, they have not yet reproduced), move from the wetlands where they were born to other areas, most often in the spring and fall. This is when we see most road-killed beavers on the roads and highways of Massachusetts.

Animals are often attracted to roads, as well. Snakes and other reptiles will bask in the warmth of the pavement early in the morning or into the evening. On the main entry into Everglades National Park one January, Kiana and I counted forty to fifty crushed snakes along the way. In Arizona, the highway that runs through Organ Pipe Cactus National Monument and into Mexico is littered with all manner of interesting, but dead, reptiles. Some mammals are drawn to roads for the salt. Still other animals come onto roads to scavenge the bodies of road-killed wildlife.

It is hard enough for most animals to get safely across a road as it is, but now we are setting up these so-called Jersey barriers along the medians of two-way, four-way, and larger highways. These barriers are the modular concrete partitions that are strung end to end along the middle of the road to keep the traffic on its proper side of the roadway. But if cars can't get through them, neither can wildlife, and so animals that make their way onto the highway get stopped in the middle and have nowhere to go. They can double back and try to return to the side from which they came, but in all likelihood they will get confused and will be pinned up against the impenetrable concrete wall. Death is the most probable outcome.

Roads and traffic are especially hard on smaller animals like amphibians (toads, frogs, salamanders) and reptiles (snakes, lizards, turtles). The species that are reliant on wetlands for reproduction but that also spend part of their life traveling overland are particularly vulnerable to vehicles as the creatures make their way across land in an attempt to move from wetland to wetland. Many species of turtles are long-lived but experience low reproductive rates and delayed sexual maturity (that is, they are not ready to breed until later in life). Hence, they need time and a somewhat stable environment to procreate. Roads are particularly hazardous to females, as they make their way to the sandy areas on land where they lay their eggs. The death of even a few of the adult breeders can have dire consequences for the local population.[16] The same concern applies to any long-lived but slowly reproducing animal—K-selected species, as ecologists say. If even a few healthy breeding adults are removed from a low-level population before they have time to reach their full breeding potential, the population suffers. The result is often local extinction. Then other individuals have difficulty recolonizing the area because they, too, have to struggle across the roads and make it past the traffic to reach new, unoccupied sites.

In addition to outright mortality caused by vehicles, the presence of roads can modify the behavior of animals.[17] Although some species may be attracted to the mowed roadside vegetation, many are repelled by the presence of roads and traffic and change their home ranges and movements in response. Researchers have documented such behavioral changes in bears, mountain lions, elk, small mammals like rodents, and grassland birds.

The most pervasive and perhaps most troubling relation between roads and wildlife, however (more so than even roadkill), is habitat fragmentation. As we have seen, roads cut up the landscape in many different ways, by opening up the forest canopy, segmenting forests, deserts, and grasslands into small separate patches, and separating the patches from one another with some barrier that is impenetrable (for some species) and hazardous (for others). Habitat fragmentation has long been a recognized problem and concern for biologists. Our extensive network of roads is a leading contributor to that problem.

We could modify some roads to help animals out. Drift fences that

run alongside roads funnel amphibians to small underground tunnels, giving them an opportunity to move across the landscape without traversing roads. Much larger underpasses or overpasses have been tried in a few places for bigger animals, with varying degrees of success.[18] Concrete Jersey barriers could be made with spaces underneath to allow medium-sized or small animals to pass through. This aid to travel wouldn't encourage animals to cross—they are going to do that anyway—but it would allow them to make it past the barrier once they did go onto the road.

Accidents are going to happen; some animals are going to get hit. Traffic is not likely to diminish or slow down in the near future; it is something we will all have to live with. If we stayed a little more aware of the situation and our surroundings, though, and if we slowed down and backed off, we might just make it where we are going without crushing the life out of some animal who just wants the same thing we want—to make it from here to there in one piece.

The female spent the summer traversing the terrain, hunting and scavenging. She has survived into her third fall, making her about two and a half years old. She was capable of breeding last year but did not. For the past year she has kept up her solitary wandering, an independent individual in a species known for independence.

This fall things were different, however. Two young males have been hanging around, moving in and out of her field of view, leaving their message markers on just about every stump and bush in the forest. Then, one fine autumn day as she lay in her field, the two of them approached from out of the adjoining woods, trotted over to her in that springy way coyotes have when they are on a mission, then simply lay down at a respectful distance. She lifted her head and stared back at the pair, as they stared at her, and then she lowered her head again onto her front paws and went back to sleep.

The two males and the female began traveling together after that. They hunted rabbits and mice, chased a few deer, explored the backyards of the nearby homes and the dumpsters behind the local line of stores. They got into

occasional squabbles over carcasses and other sources of food, but by and large they spent their early autumn days together in harmony, a pack of three. They denned up in a loose group, each one finding its own spot to curl up and sleep, and then came together again when it was time to travel the woods and fields and neighborhoods in the continual search for something to eat. They ventured across a parking lot at the local elementary school one morning but dashed away to take cover nearby as soon as they heard the loud, agitated voices of people in the area.

One raw fall day, as the wind whipped through the trees and began to blow gold and red leaves to the ground, the female heard deep-throated growls and high-pitched yips, the sound of jaws popping and a struggle in the underbrush. The commotion went on for many minutes before it died down. From deeper in the woods the slightly larger of the two males emerged, the fur around his neck and one side of his head wet with heavy spittle, and a small red gash running down the left side of his muzzle just under the eye. He lay down some distance from her, breathing heavily, and she laid her head back down on her front paws, looking up at him from the top of her eyes. After a moment they rose together and trotted off to the southeast.[19]

CHAPTER 8

A Trilogy of Tolerable Nuisances, Parts 2 and 3

Light and Noise

In language and landscape, Australia is a continent steeped in poetry. You hear it in the accents of its people, both aboriginal and immigrant: in the way they speak and in the names they give to things. You see that poetry etched into the earth—along the coasts, on the forested hillsides, and beyond, farther into the desert outback. The poetry becomes performing art when you step into a gum tree forest at night. All is sound and movement, for a good deal of Australia's native fauna is nocturnal by nature and comes out to perform when the sun goes down.

In a spotted gum forest in southern Queensland I look up through the reticulated canopy to see stars twinkling now and then, and I know the sky is clear and the weather will be good tomorrow. The glow of early moonlight against the tree trunks makes them look like marble columns, giving the forest structure, like ancient architecture.

A chorus of flying foxes comes alive with a great squawking and flapping of wings. The bats are readying themselves for their nightly foray. The forest falls silent for a moment on their departure, until you hear the rustling of animals that live in the trunks of trees during the day—in cavities, as we call them in North America, or hollows, as they call them in Australia—but emerge now, at night, to eat foliage or lick tree sap.

Kevin Wormington, a graduate student at the University of Queensland, aims his spotlight beam at the sound, while Damien Moloney, one of his advisers, calls out the names of creatures as they emerge from the trees: brush-tail possum, yellow-bellied glider, sugar glider. Some, like the feather-tailed glider, are diminutive, mincing and delicate in their movements among the branches. Others, like the greater glider, are so big you wonder how they fit through the hole from which they just emerged.

We search for the bits of reflective tape that Kevin put on the trees earlier to mark his transects, and we cruise along quietly, stopping at prearranged stations to listen for several minutes in the dark. After a pause at each station, Kev lights up the canopy of branches in the search for more arboreal marsupials. Within several hours Kevin and Damien have the data they need, and we make our way back to camp.

On the way we shine our lights at a field along the edge of the forest just in time to see the head of a wallaby popping up and down above the vegetation as it flees the area. Wallabies belong to a group of mammals that make their way across the landscape by hopping—by saltatory locomotion, as a zoologist would call it. That same zoologist would say that animals like wallabies hop because it is a more efficient mode of transportation for their lifestyle than walking. They expend less energy to travel greater distances, and thus the behavior is cost-effective, energy-conserving, adaptive.[1] A poet-naturalist might say that wallabies hop to be different, in an expression of joy and grace that serves as a reminder to humans of the beauty of the world and the glory of nature. Most days I don't really see the difference in the two lines of thought, poetic and ecological, but tonight I'm just curious to see what we might discover next in a land where everything is new to me.

A boobook owl flies across in front of us and lands in a tree. We get a good look at it in the spotlight, a small brown owl with lightly etched markings around its eyes, giving it an intense and studious look. A bit farther along we hear a subtle rustling in the grassy undergrowth and we turn quiet and stealthy. Kevin wields his spotlight like a pistol as we sneak up on the spot from which the noise is coming. Kev aims and opens up the beam. Caught in the light is a creature that I think cannot be from earth. It is somewhat familiar in its form and structure, but entirely new to me in its size and movements. It looks like a giant mouse and a miniature kangaroo all at once. It freezes for a moment in the sudden flood of light but then continues with what it was doing, taking small hops from here to there, digging at the earth and grabbing at vegetation with its small front paws. I hear Kevin whisper, "Bettong." "Yes," says Damien, "A rufous bettong." I had only recently become aware that there were animals called bettongs. Now I am looking at one, as it moves to the edge of the spotlight beam—a small macropod, similar in form to kangaroos, wallabies, and potoroos, but different in size. The creature digs in the dirt, pulling up what look like tubers or fat roots. After a while, careful to respect its space, we give it a wide berth as we loop around and continue on our way.

At camp we crawl into our bedrolls to the sound of a barking owl, hooting down the intruders in its territory, and I fall asleep thinking about the rufous bettong going about its business, blending in with the forest, melting into the darkness. 🐝

It is a late summer night, just past midnight. I find myself still wakeful, reluctant to "give up the day" as my wife has always said about those long summer days she spent in Alaska, when the light never really leaves and you want to stay up . . . puttering around, getting more chores done. We called it tundra time when I worked up in Churchill. But here it is dark, and the sky above Western Massachusetts is littered with stars. I wander over to the edge of our little field. The dogs have followed me out, suspecting that I may be up to something interesting, and we all water the yard where the field meets the woods.

Looking up, I think of the time I spent in southern Arizona. The clear skies and dry desert air always allowed an amazing view of the stars at night. Camping in the desert, visiting my friend Wild Bill near the Mexican border, where we'd step outside before turning in, or taking forays with Ki up into the mountains would reveal a night sky packed with stars, the Milky Way like a cloud stretching high across the heavens. The lack of humidity or haze certainly contributes to the astounding view of stars in the southwestern United States, but so does the ability to get some distance out into the desert and away from the concentration of lights that exists in cities like Tucson.

A city dweller might not even know that there were stars out there, especially in a place like Las Vegas. There, the trade has been made: the modern blaze of neon and halogen in exchange for an ancient and humble twinkling of stars. In Las Vegas you call all those bright lights excitement; the International Dark-Sky Association (IDA), the world's first organization to actively fight this kind of glare, calls it light pollution.[2] The IDA defines light pollution as "any adverse effect of man-made light including sky glow, glare, light trespass, and light clutter," most often emanating from big metropolitan centers. Once again we find that what happens in Vegas does not really stay in Vegas; it reaches well beyond the borders of the city, out into the desert and even up into space.

Tucson actually has ordinances designed to keep down the city lights, for the benefit of the astronomers who flock there like pilgrims to a holy place. The first "lighting code" went into effect in 1972, when the city moved to reduce streetlight glare and limit lighting of businesses and homes. Then, in 1999, a major victory was won when Pima

County rejected the idea of a $900 million development consisting of six hundred homes and a large commercial district on a former ranch, because of concerns that the new lights might increase sky brightness by 8 to 14 percent.[3]

As a wildlife biologist, I envy the success professional astronomers and amateur stargazers have had in halting sprawl at least temporarily, with the blessing of county officials and the support of the community to boot. Let us remember, though, that theirs is space-related "hard science," with many million dollars' worth of equipment and complex mathematical equations to back it. We have been educated to recognize that space exploration is not free ("No bucks, no Buck Rogers" to quote the astronaut in *The Right Stuff*[4]), and the public generally agrees that space exploration is important, whether we do it from the confines of earth or actually go up there.

We still don't think of ecology in terms of costs and benefits; we always assume that the things nature provides on our home planet are mostly free.[5] Regardless of that difference in expectations, I say good for the astronomers; their success is our success. As a wildlife biologist, however, I also realize that the success is probably only temporary, as do they. During the debate over light pollution in Tucson, the astronomer Craig Foltz was quoted in the magazine *Science* as stating, "With all this growth, you realize you can only stay so long in a place. And that's too bad."[6] You could put that on my tombstone, if it was all right with Craig.

We have been aware for some time of light pollution as affecting our view of the night sky.[7] But now we are finding out more about the effects of massive amounts of artificial light on some species of plants and animals. In fact, ecologists have drawn a distinction between "astronomical light pollution," which obscures the view of the night sky, and "ecological light pollution," which affects the behavior of wild animals and natural communities.[8] Ecological light pollution comes from buildings, towers, vehicles, streetlights, security lights—anything that produces artificial light and burns throughout the night. It emanates from virtually the entire developed world, and more and more from the developing world. The pollution is truly global in its extent and influence.

Humans have been aware that light affects animals ever since the first person observed a moth being drawn to a flame. Such effects of light remained restricted to a very small scale—the local moths and other insects flew toward a fire or candle flame and some of them died, but the impact was not on entire populations. With the proliferation of artificial lights all over the world, however, circumstances have changed for lots of wild animals. As with everything involving people, it is the numbers that count: there are so many of us now that even our lights are having an impact on our world.

Artificial light can alter the behavior and biological cycles of some animals.[9] Birds are particularly affected, especially during migration, when lights can disorient and confuse them. At times large numbers of birds collide with light towers. For some sea turtles, bright lights along the coast discourage females from coming ashore to lay their eggs. On beaches where eggs are laid, lights can attract the hatchlings and draw them away from the ocean. Lights can even cause some salamanders and frogs to change their behavior: they stay hidden for more of the night, when normally they would be out feeding or singing during that brief period of spring when conditions are right for procreation. Fireflies alter their reproductive behavior, and untold numbers of other nocturnal insects are drawn to lights and die. The effects on mammals are less clear, but who knows what the introduction of artificial lighting does to the behavior of the hundreds of nocturnal species normally active during periods of darkness? Apparently even certain processes in plants, such as flowering and leaf fall, can be altered by the ever-present glow of artificial lights. Of course, some species are always ready to take advantage of changing conditions. Some bats, particularly those which use long-range echolocation and fly fast and straight, and some small lizards, particularly non-native species, exploit the situation to capture insects around streetlamps.[10]

As little time as we spend considering how light affects animals, we may think even less about how it affects us. Scientists estimate that less than half of all Americans live in areas dark enough to cause the eyes to make the transition from cone vision (which we use to sense color) to rod vision (rods are more sensitive to light). Indeed, according to some estimates, well over nine-tenths of Americans live with some form of light pollution, and two-thirds of us can no longer see the Milky Way from where we live.[11] Dr. Michael Rosbash, an investigator with the Howard Hughes Medical Institute, says, "When an animal is exposed to constant, intense light, the internal clock goes haywire, losing all sense of night and day. Fruit flies exhibit the same reaction, and humans are predicted to respond similarly."[12]

To be sure, artificial light improves our lives enormously, in countless ways, but you have to ask yourself, Is this yet another example of too much of a good thing? Do we need to have the number and intensity of lights that we do? Does everything have to be lit up? Does our innate fear of the dark predicate our deep-seated desire to obliterate it completely, like wilderness, like predators, like risk itself? We so desire to live in a supersafe world that we have all but forgotten what it is like to wander in the dark using our four other senses and to let the world have its night.

The glow, glare, and trespass of lights have changed our view of the natural world. It is not really something we notice anymore, not until we are on a vacation that takes us away from it all and we see what the sky can look like on a clear night. By now, however, we consider that view an anomaly: the stars just aren't visible like this at home. I don't even think we realize that they are there, up above our suburban neighborhoods; it's just that we can no longer see them. It hardly even registers as a tolerable nuisance for most of us, this washing-out of the stars, but it is a hard thing for those who know what we are missing. It is a subtle sadness, not seeing the Milky Way from home. And who knows what the absence of stars does to our perspective, to our understanding of the universe and our place in it?

It's very early morning, predawn, and I am lying awake at about my usual time, 4 A.M. It is an uncharacteristically cool night for mid-August, and a sweet breeze carries in through the open window with the first suggestion of a coming fall. It is still dark, but I take in sounds as if they were the morning light filtering in over the eastern horizon. They are weightless and comforting sounds, from both within and outside our bedroom. I can hear the soft, regular breathing of my wife beside me and the occasional twitching of the dogs on their beds. From a distance a train whistle floats in on the air, a sound that always takes me back to childhood, when from across the river I could hear the night trains, carrying their freight and making their runs from the suburbs into the city and back again. The breeze rustles through the leaves, and from a long way away I hear the piercing one-note call of a barred owl.[13]

I have been blessed and cursed with better-than-average hearing. While others in my family have been robbed of some of their ability to hear, I seem to have retained more than my fair share. My eyesight has never been the best, and now that I am in my fifties, it and other faculties are in decline, but my hearing has stayed with me. My hearing is a blessing when I am out in nature or lying awake on a still night at home, when there are nothing but the soft, intimate sounds of the world to be heard. It is a curse if the neighbors are acting up or if I'm someplace where the traffic is loud. At night errant noises are more likely to keep me awake than worries over finances or job performance, or any of those other troubles that make people restless at night in our modern world.

When we first moved into this house, we were faced with replacing the water and electrical lines, all of which needed to be buried underground. It was a fairly big undertaking, given that our house is set back three hundred feet from the road and the lines needed to be at least four feet down. It took a goodly amount of backhoe work; we called it our own Big Dig, after the highly publicized megaproject in Boston. The job actually went smoothly, but it took a couple of days, and so for one night we lived without running water or electricity. It was April of the year and still cool. That evening we made supper on the woodstove and ate in the kitchen by candlelight. We marveled at how quiet it was in the house. Noises that we had grown accustomed to were noticeable by their absence, and we realized that in our normally pretty quiet neighborhood, the house itself emitted all kinds of sounds. The refrig-

erator, the water heater and water pump, the computer, the television, and all the other electronic things that hum in the background were now silent, as was the immediate world around us. I slept like a baby that night. We vowed to turn off all the power to the house every once in a while, so that we could enjoy the light of candles, the warmth of the woodstove, and the quiet, but we haven't done it since.

Noise is a personal issue. All sound is relative. What is a comfort to me is likely to be an annoyance to others, and certainly the opposite is true. That night train whistle can be pleasant if it comes from a distance and conjures up childhood memories, but it's a nightmare if the tracks run too close to your house. The call of an owl sets my heart at ease, whereas it sets another person's nerves on edge. If that owl happens to pounce on a rabbit in the early evening hours, the screams of the victim will freak out most people. To me cries like that are a reassuring sound—nature is still at work in the neighborhood.

The noise that most directly impinges on our lives in cities and suburbs has been called an "unwanted product of our technological civilization." It has also been termed a scourge of the modern world, a pervasive and intense antagonism, a global issue, and the third jeopardy of environmental pollutants, after air and water pollution. It has been described as that "ever-increasing din that disturbs our sleep, interrupts our conversation, creates anxiety and annoyance, and sometimes damages hearing." It is said that unexpected or unwanted noise can cause our pupils to dilate, our skin to pale, our mucous membranes to dry out, and our adrenal glands to "explode [with] secretions," causing "individual cognitive dissonance" as well as "mass societal neuroses," making people more irritable and more prone to irrational and neurotic behavior.[14] None of this can be good.

It less clear how noise affects wildlife. I've heard that black bears in some places will stay away from the edge of roads when the traffic is loud. In Tucson my graduate student Charlene Webster and I changed our plans for studying roadrunners in the city (an "urban wildlife" project) when we realized that we couldn't hear the roadrunner's territorial "coo" calls because of the city noise. That we couldn't hear them affected our ability to do our study, but if a roadrunner cannot hear other roadrunners, it could have implications for the roadrunner population in the area. In fact, researchers have found that some city birds alter their songs to be heard above the din of their urban surroundings, an amazing example of adaptation in the face of an ever-changing environment.[15] It also appears that birds with higher-pitched songs are more abundant along roads where traffic is loud than birds with lower-pitched songs, an indication that the first group is less susceptible to noise pollution.[16] We already know that loud noises, such as those resulting from military activity, can influence the behavior and movements of some species of wildlife.[17] Scientists speculate that with increasing industrialization and development of the Arctic, the noise may have a negative effect on polar bears, which have particularly acute hearing.[18] What's more, researchers report that noise in urban areas can vary by neighborhood. The volume of sound, being influenced by the structure of the urban environment (for example, by the hard vertical surfaces of buildings, which can deflect and amplify sound), will follow predictable patterns during the day. These influence communication in animal communities, but some animals can learn to adapt to the changes.[19]

Of all the tolerable nuisances, noise is the final frontier in suburban and urban living. We have yet to recognize and admit how much noise really does bother us, no matter how hard we try just to live with it. We lament the crowdedness and congestion of urban and suburban life, the lack of privacy and the smell of exhaust, the closing-in of neighborhoods and the infilling of the last remnants of open space. We complain about the loudest of noises, such as jackhammers and jumbo jets and car horns, but most noises we simply try to ignore and live with. Many of us can tune out just about anything. So we put up with the sound of lawn mowers, leaf blowers, throbbing stereos, garage rock bands, errant car alarms, barking dogs, the hum of rubber on pavement, the raised voices of neighbors, and the thump of air-compressed nail guns as they drive home the fasteners on a new suburban home.

What is odd is how aware of noise we become when it is absent. It takes the quiet of the desert, the woods in winter, a freak snowstorm in the city, or a break in the electrical service to make us realize how much noise we live with.

The female and the male roamed the hills of central Massachusetts for the remainder of the fall and into early winter. They had gravitated to an area, roughly two miles square, on the edge of a little town, the countryside around a mix of fields and marshes and woodlots. Homes and small farms dotted the landscape, through which a river curled its way, frozen in places, free-flowing in others, depending on the gradient and the amount of sunlight that filtered through the bare tree branches. On clear days the snow and ice glinted like starlight in the weak winter sun.

During the second week in February the female began to show a profound change in behavior. The male, who had been waiting patiently for the past several days, was well aware of the female's newfound interest in him. The scent of her had kept him in close attendance, although his first advances were sharply rebuffed. The female's demeanor had now changed. For the next ten days they would couple and uncouple, and for the next few weeks the two were inseparable. They hunted together and slept nestled close and searched for a place that she would deem suitable.[20]

CHAPTER 9

Home Ownership and Other Near-Death Experiences

🐾 Winter is my season. In cold and snow I'm in my element. Having lived in places—beautiful places—that have no real winter, I've learned that I could live there for a time, but that they would never be home. Home to me has four seasons, winter and the other three.

It is mid-February now, and if it is winter I want, I got it, because everything around me is buried deep in snow, and it is cold enough to be comfortable in three layers of thick clothing: long johns, wool pants and shirt, insulated coveralls. I am snowmobiling up a Forest Service road in the heart of the Okanogan National Forest in north-central Washington State. I bring the Polaris Long Track to a stop on the trail, where it overlooks a deep valley. I leave the engine running and move like an astronaut in full regalia as I make my way to the edge of the ridge. I aim the telemetry antenna down into the valley and listen for the beeps that tell me a collared lynx is hunting this area . . .

The northern Cascade Mountains of the Pacific Northwest get real winter. Deep snow. Cold. The day dawns late and fades early, but what daylight there is shines on a glistening world of high white peaks and snow-burdened trees. And in that white mountain wilderness, in the middle of the fourth and best season, the snow-covered slopes are crisscrossed with tracks left by intrepid wildlife. Coyotes, mule deer, spruce grouse, porcupines, elk, foxes, bears, and ravens leave their mark and make their play in the game of survival, with winter as the rubber match.

Among the best at the game of survival are lynx, bobcats, and mountain lions—all the wild felids that northern North America has to offer. During this winter in the northern Cascades I got to know all three, not so much as fur and flesh but as prints in snow and ice—four round toes and a central pad in a two-step pattern, the tracks aligned perfectly in a trail through the forest, down the logging road, across the frozen meadow, over the ridge, and into the next valley.

The prints of cats are all the same. The tiniest house cat has the paws of a Siberian tiger, only smaller. The cats of the Cascades display the same relationship. Mountain lions are the largest—no mistaking the size or misunderstanding the power. Lynx are next—theirs is the familiar cat track with a twist, caused by the unusual amount of fur around the toes that aids them in their pursuit of hares in deep snow. Bobcats are smallest of the three—as delicate as any tabby but as efficient as any leopard.

I followed a lion trail down a valley one day. At one point, reflecting a moment of haste or pursuit, the animal's trail ended in front of a pile of brush. As far as I could tell, cougars could fly, because the tracks left the earth and did not show up on the other side until I was thirty feet downslope, where I saw them again in the snow.

I followed lynx tracks through a stand of lodgepole pines one afternoon. It was tough going because dozens of trees had fallen and lay stacked and crossed like a box of spilled matchsticks. The trail wandered through the trees and then appeared atop one of the logs and following along, turned onto another and another log, and so on. At the edge of the stand the cat had taken a seat in the snow for a moment before going on, into the forest.

I followed the trail of a bobcat around the base of a rimrock cliff one morning. The deeper snow higher up in the mountains was for lynx; bobcats occupied these lower reaches and blind valleys. The prints were outlined clearly in the wet snow where the trail curved around the edge of the cliff. I followed the tracks around a corner, then perched on a ledge that overlooked the low sweep of the valley below, until I reached a stretch of bare rock. There the cat's prints faded away, leaving no trace of its passing . . .

In a minute I hear what I am listening for, the steady cadence of beeps that tells me one of our collared animals is in the pine and fir on the upper slopes of the valley below. As I return to the snowmobile, I find an odd kind of comfort in its throaty idling engine, indicating that it is still running and able to get me home. The sign at the nearby trail junction that points back the other way reads, "Conconully, 75," showing the direction and the distance to the little town where my Forest Service cabin waits. It is a long way back. I wonder if I really could make it if the engine did decide to quit. Do I have enough food and enough stamina to save myself from a long winter night on the mountain, staving off frostbite and hypothermia? Risk of some sort is often involved in fieldwork and is always accepted as part of the deal by field biologists. The skis that stick out the back of the snowmobile are my way out if I do have engine trouble or some other mechanical failure that I am not able to fix, but it would be a long, long ski back. Would I be able to do it? I hop on the Long Track, rev the engine, and make a loop at the junction where the two roads cross and head back down the mountain. Today I will not have to find out: the snowmobile carries me back home.

I have had maybe three near-death experiences in my life so far. None of them were real cliff-hangers. They were, instead, more like delayed near-death experiences—the kind of thing that occurs to you hours or even days later, when you are sitting around and you think, "I really could have died then."

The first was when I went over a small (about twelve-foot) waterfall in a canoe on a river in Oregon. I got flipped out at the top of the falls and was swept helplessly over and down. All I remember is that moments later I opened my eyes to green water with thin strings of bubbles rising all around me. What I didn't know at the time was that I was in a plunge pool and that people had died in this very spot because the force of the water held them down until they drowned. Not knowing this, I felt strangely calm as I tried swimming toward the surface, which appeared as a dim circle of yellow light above me. I swam upward for what seemed a long time, expecting to break the surface at any moment. When I kept *not* reaching the surface, I kept on swimming, not feeling tired but thinking, This is taking too long. At some point, probably only seconds later, it occurred to me that I was not going to make it. I didn't panic at the thought; it was more a feeling like, "Oh well, time's up." At that moment, however, I surfaced, made it over to a rock, and crawled up on my belly, gasping for air like a carp in the shallows.

The second instance occurred during one of my summers up at Cape Churchill, when I was working as a field biologist on the tundra. One bright, sunny day in mid-July, when the fieldwork was at a low ebb and we had time on our hands, I grabbed my camera and thinking I would spend a good part of the day photographing tundra wildflowers, headed south along the camp ridge. I walked a couple of miles from camp, lying on my belly from time to time to take pictures, and after several hours made my slow way back. I had no sooner made it back to camp and casually latched the gate, when I heard a noise behind me. I turned and saw two young polar bears—young but close to fully grown—just outside the fence. The bears had obviously followed me back to camp. It was a warm day, and I surmised that they had been in the willows by the lake, taking in the shade and lolling in the cool water. They may even have seen me leave camp; maybe they had been watching me the whole time I was out on my naive picture-taking tour. Bears leave people alone more often than not, but if they decide differently, it can mean trouble. It was just not the day that my time was up, not the day for them to come after me . . . cutting off my retreat . . . batting me about, like cats with a ball of twine.

The third story is from my time in Alaska. It is the one that sticks with me the most, because at the end of it I read an account of what could have been me, alive no longer. It was midspring and my friend Bob and I were driving to McCarthy, a small former mining camp and now tourist spot on the Kennicott River in the Wrangall–Saint Elias National Preserve. There was still some snow around, and we were hitting patches of compacted snow and ice that we were calling miniglaciers. We were in Bob's little two-wheel-drive pickup, but we were making good time and traversing the miniglaciers with no trouble, until we got to within a few miles of McCarthy.

At that point we came face to face with the biggest miniglacier of all. We pulled over and turned off the engine, then climbed out to assess the situation. After two minutes of silent looking and five minutes of conversation, we decided to go for it. We got back in, and Bob hit the gas and let it fly. He got the truck up on the ice and was making progress, but pretty soon the back end started to fishtail, a bit at first, then more, until we were sliding over to the bank. I yelled for him to stop just as the rear wheels slid over, and we were saved from going down the side by nothing more than a small clump of saplings. Long Lake lay below us, looking both spectacularly beautiful and alarmingly menacing.

We were stuck now. The rear wheel was up against the trees, and even a modest touch of the gas would send the tire spinning helplessly on the glare ice. I looked up and down the road—no one coming in either direction. We had seen only one other vehicle along the twenty-something-mile stretch we had driven so far. It was getting to be late in the day, and I started thinking we might be here for a while—overnight anyway. I quickly went over in my mind what we had in the truck: one candy bar, two half-empty water bottles, a hammer, and an orange. Not good.

So we set to doing all we could think to do. Bob put snow cables on the rear wheels and chipped away at the ice in front of the tires with his small hammer, while I gathered stout branches to build a barrier to keep us from sliding off the road and down the bank if we did manage to urge the truck forward. We struggled for quite a while, until Bob had had enough, got into the truck, and gunned it for all its four-cylinder engine was worth. The left rear wheel slammed against my make-shift barrier, but it held. The tires caught, and he shot across the rest of the ice like a pea from a blowgun. We had made it out.

The chilling part came three weeks later. I was back in Oregon when I got a short letter and a brief newspaper clipping from Bob, who was still in Alaska. Apparently, a week before, two guys were traveling down this same road and made it as far as the same patch of snow. Their small truck slid on the ice, too, but they never had a chance to get out and assess the situation. They missed the saplings, went over the steep bank, and rolled down into the lake below. They were found in thirty feet of water a day or two later, their seatbelts still on.

The riskiest thing I do in life now is probably work on the house. Actually, driving is worse, but climbing a ladder or messing around up on the roof are activities that probably threaten my life more than anything other than driving. Working with power tools also poses some risk, but more of grievous injury than of actual death. Some four hundred thousand Americans were injured by power tools and workshop equipment in 2000. Falls, including those from ladders and scaffolding, killed almost twenty thousand people in the United States in 2004.[1] Add to those dangers burns, tripping and slipping, hitting electric wires with aluminum ladders, getting foreign objects in your eyes in the midst of performing any number of tasks (and not wearing goggles), croaking with a snow shovel in your hands, getting bitten by the dog or cat, stepping on rusty nails, and on and on, and home begins to look like a pretty hazardous place. Plenty of things around the house can hurt you. It's a jungle out there—in the yard, up on the roof, down in the basement, or out in the garage.

Most of us think it is worth the risk, though. Our houses mean a lot to us. In fact, there's no mistaking how important having a house and a home is to most Americans. Home ownership is one of the key elements of the great American dream. I am sure it is the same for many people around the world.

I talk with an acquaintance at work, and being both engaged in long-term remodeling efforts, we update each other on our progress. It is always slow going, but she speaks of her house and land with such reverence that it has really made an impression on me. From her description, it is a modest home on a couple of acres, but she has worked hard all her life for her place, and now both the house and the yard are close to where she wants them to be. It gives her such joy and peace, in the way only a home can, that it is touching.

I talk with another old friend, and we exchange complaints and laments over the never-ending list of remodeling projects we have going on (is there a pattern here?), but he talks about his house as if it were a close relative. He worries about it when it is ill (has a leaky roof or a crack in the siding) and does what he can to nurse it back to health. He shows the same affection for it as one would for an aging parent. My cousin Donny lives in Eastern Massachusetts, and we talk every week and mark our progress in life by how much we have accomplished on our home improvement plans. Sometimes it seems life barely moves forward, and the projects creep along at an unbearably slow pace; other times we advance by leaps and bounds.

Real estate agents and loan officials are always reminding us that a house is, for most people, the biggest investment they will make in their lives. We really don't need an agent or a banker to tell us this. We put everything we have into our homes—heart, soul, and cash. Our houses arguably absorb more of our money, time, and energy than almost any other thing in life. We worry about them when we are away or when something—the furnace or the plumbing—is on the fritz. We feel good when everything is working or when we get a chance to update. Putting on an addition or remodeling the kitchen is a major lifetime event for most people, filled with trials and triumphs, like most human endeavors. Even a fresh coat of paint for the living room is invigorating, like a splash of fresh cool water on our faces in the morning.

Still, our involvement with property can be a love-hate relationship. It takes a lot of effort to keep up a house and a yard, and most of us give up more weekends to that end than we care to acknowledge. I fell into that pattern when Ki and I purchased our house in New Salem, Massachusetts, some years ago now. It was a neat place, a gambrel-style house with dormers and a nice front porch, wood floors, and a big central brick fireplace. The place was tucked back off the road and nestled into twenty-two acres of woodland with a small, unnamed creek that we ended up calling Winter Creek, because one of us, at least, likes winter and because it all but quits flowing in the summer.

Perhaps best of all, the town is perched on the northwestern corner of the Quabbin Reservoir, a 120,000-acre preserve that is the major source of water for the city of Boston and many of its surrounding suburbs. The reservoir was created in the 1930s and 1940s, and today it can hold some 400 billion gallons of fresh, clear water when it is at full capacity. I grew up on Quabbin water without knowing it. Quabbin water is known as some of the purest water in the country, and the land around the water is managed to protect the water supply. As such, the Quabbin watershed forms an incredibly large chunk of habitat for many wild animals: deer, moose, bears, fishers, eagles, ospreys, loons, thrushes, warblers, owls, woodcock, grouse, turtles, salamanders, dragonflies, butterflies and fritillaries, and on and on. The place is rich in all manner of wildlife and (although there are some restrictions) incredible recreational opportunities for the citizens of the Commonwealth. Some have called it an accidental wilderness.[2] That is not a bad name for it, after all, especially in a place like southern New England where little land remains that is not subject to human use of one kind or another. The Quabbin is a precious jewel for Massachusetts, and the two great lobes of its waters lie like a misshapen heart in the center of the state. I go to bed tonight thankful that it is there and I am lucky enough to have it as a neighbor.

As nice as our house was, it still wasn't enough for me, so I set about making plans to build an addition and expand the smallish kitchen. I think it was the builder's heritage in me and my need to work on something physical and tangible that spurred me on in the beginning. One winter, then, I spent a good deal of time reading about foundations and framing techniques and drawing up plans. We were going to have a nice-sized room where the kitchen would transition into a living room—a great room—with lots of windows looking out onto our little meadow and the woods beyond. It was going to be good, it was going to be fun, and it was going to take only a year or two to complete.

I won't bore you with the details. Suffice it to say that I am still working on it, five years later. We've accomplished a lot, but the final finishing touches seem to be taking forever. As one neighbor, who is going through the same thing with her husband, quipped, "I am learning that trim is optional."

But no matter. A true loving relationship is always a work in progress, right? So it is for most of us with our houses. There's a reason those big-box discount home centers take up so much of the landscape, and a reason home improvement shows like *This Old House* are so popular. This need to establish a home range, this nesting effort, this constant attention to our den site is a powerful motivating incentive in many of us—like a force of nature. Ernst Haeckel, the zoologist who coined the word "ecology," was right to take it from the Greek for "house."

So I work away on our addition, spending more time and more money than I originally intended, just the way everyone says you will. Mostly I enjoy it, and I do get a great deal of satisfaction when something is finished and I can step back and look at it. Still, I sometimes long for the days when I could put everything I owned into my small pickup truck and I led a nomad's existence. But Ki and I love our home, and we look forward to the day when it will be finished, knowing full well that it never will be.

The importance of a home is a deep-seated human trait that we have carried into our modern lives. And it is a worthy endeavor to build a sound, safe structure or to restore an older house, to improve upon what you have, to care for a building like one of the family. I just wish we all could carry the passion and love and care that we show for the buildings in which we live to the land and air and water that surround and support them. I wish our nation as a whole had the same *This Old House* kind of enthusiasm for the natural environment that we have for the built environment. It is every bit as important to your immediate well-being as paying the mortgage and keeping water out of the basement. Without all the things the earth provides, the place in which you live will no longer be the sweet and comforting place you know as home. The real estate agents are wrong: your house is only your second biggest investment in your life. Your environment is your first.

Despite all that we have learned and are learning about our environment, we still tend to stick our heads in the sand. We continue on our merry way, building, spending, consuming. It is certainly true that the tide of building has slowed with the recent worries about energy prices and the economy, but it is economic incentives that continue to motivate us, rather than a change in philosophy. I wonder what our lifestyle choices would be if we could successfully switch to a superabundant and free source of energy. Would we say, hey, things were a bit out of control when oil was cheap? Would we curb our appetite for energy consumption if our cars ran on batteries and our homes were heated and powered by the sun? And despite the economic troubles of the moment, are there lessons to be learned about our spending habits and our priorities when the economy does turn back around?

So, I still worry about our propensity for more and bigger things. I fret over development and sprawl and the loss of acreage, the fragmentation of habitat, the degradation of biodiversity. This is the burden that I carry with me as a product of suburbia and as one of the many whose lifestyle has outstripped the ability of the planet to support it. It induces a helpless feeling, especially in my home state of Massachusetts. Massachusetts is small and vulnerable, with its high density of people and its proximity to huge cities and their sprawling suburbs, and with its lack of federally protected lands, unlike so many states in the West.

For much of the developed world now, it seems the only way to deal with the rapid growth—more homes, more people, more traffic, more noise—is to find a way to tolerate it . . . unless, of course, you are rich and can afford to "own the view," as Frank Lloyd Wright allegedly suggested. That is really what it all comes down to anyway—money. Americans have bought into the economic-growth model of life lock, stock, and barrel. Sure, we are in a real estate market slump for the moment, largely of our own making, and we moan about it as if it will go on forever, but it will not. We have become convinced that building more homes and buying more things not only benefit our economy but exemplify the good life. Our consumption increases the tax base, which we think will boost the amount in the operating budgets of our towns, spread out the tax burden, and give us more services for less money. Yet taxes go up, continually and dramatically. We are pretty blind to the fact that property taxes climb when more homes bring more people, who need more services. We all call for better roads, enhanced capacity to deal with the mounds of trash, more power lines, more water, more and more of everything. In the meantime, open space, breathing room, quiet, and even a small sense of solitude evaporate like dew on the asphalt roofs on the newly built homes which have rapidly replaced the fields and woodlots that gave our towns character, along with the pleasant feeling that used to be associated with the word "hometown."

In the foreseeable future I worry that our little town will cease to be a quaint, scenic, peaceful Western Massachusetts community. I can see the first tides of development flowing from the south up Route 202, and from the eastern shore, along Route 2 from Boston. I wonder if this place has any chance of withstanding the assault on two fronts. A full tide of development will hit us, with the force of syzygy behind it. I've seen it before; it starts with the building of a few new homes on the more accessible and available lots, but it quickly spreads out to encompass everything. The building, when it starts, will be rapid and unstoppable.

When a spurt in development does occur, we will be told we are lucky: our property values will increase. Our investment in our house will pay off big. In the meantime, the noise and the congestion and the taxes will go up, as the sense of community and tranquility go down. I am an optimist most of the time, but unbridled development creates a periodic pessimism in me that causes me to sink as low as the water table will in the next few years, as more and more wells are dug. I felt that sinking feeling a few short years ago, as new building sites sprang up along the entire length of our road.

The recent posting of more "Lot for Sale" signs in the neighborhood depresses me; the feeling of helplessness to do anything about it angers me. I get into heated discussions with other people in town, or more often I just come home raving about it to my wife. I let the whole topic get to me from time to time, to the point where it is clear that I need to get away for a bit. So I grab my snowshoes and head for the closest thing to wilderness that Massachusetts has to offer, the Quabbin. I am underdressed for the cold, but I don't care. I know the walking will warm me up soon enough. I shove a candy bar into my breast pocket and leave the camera and binoculars behind. They tend to annoy me at times, anyway. I wish I could take the dogs, but I know the signs say no, so I don't. I leave the water bottle in the truck. I'll eat snow. I don't really care what the guidebooks tell you about going prepared. To hell with that—let them find me days later, sitting stiff and frozen against a boulder down by the water, frost covering my beard, middle finger raised in a final frozen salute to the twin gods of progress and sprawl. I strap on the shoes and wade into the snow, fleeing the world of town planners and building developers and real estate agents, pursuing a "primitive and unconfined type of recreation" with a grim look on my face.

I am no more than fifty feet down the trail when I feel the stress seeping out of me. It is same effect that the woods—or the desert or the prairies or the tundra or the marshes—always have on me. Water bubbles quietly below the ice of a creek along the trail . . . the sweet

sound of running water. A small band of chickadees are the first to greet me . . . flitting wings, singsong calls. I pause and look at their perfect little forms as they gather in the twigs just above me.

As my head clears, I see what so often I don't want to see, the dichotomy in me that is all too obvious. No one told me I had to build the big addition onto my house. No one told me that I had to embrace the luxuries of modern life, accept the big paycheck, buy the stuff, drive the car, and fly in the planes. This is like all the hard things in life—arguments, failures, divorce—acknowledging my role in it is not easy. But part of me realizes the necessity of staring into the face of these uncomfortable realities and seeing my own reflection. I kick at the snow and continue down the trail, thinking maybe I need to calm down and make some apologies when I get home.

For the rest of the day I enjoy being where I am. It is cold and quiet, a world of horizontal white layerings of snow and vertical gray trunks of trees. Bare branches mingle in perfect random patterns against a partly sunny sky, as clouds move by and build up at a constant rate of speed. The wind picks up, then dies down, and soon it begins to snow.

I think of how great my wife is—how much we like our house, how much we like our town. I know when I am done my truck will be waiting, three-quarters of a tank of gas and a working heater, to get me back to a warm home and a good supper, border collies waiting in the driveway, chickens ready to be put up for the night.

For now I appreciate the Quabbin for what it is, the nature of winter, the presence of the woods, and, maybe most of all, the remnants of the gentle landscape that is Massachusetts. I am fully aware of the "world of wounds" of which Aldo Leopold spoke. I have some sense of what it means to love a thing that is hard to love, and yet to love it just the same.[3]

🐾 As they roam throughout their territory, the female and her mate have started to investigate holes in the ground, spaces under tree roots, and small caves in boulder cliffs. They travel side by side, spending much of their time mousing in the deep, soft snow of the meadow. It looks like slow-motion play as they spring into the air, then remain suspended above the ground for a moment, ready for the pounce, all four legs poised, but it is serious business, despite the look of a self-satisfied grin as they chomp down another vole.

One afternoon she stops in the middle of hunting in a nearby field and wanders over to a steep bank near the edge of the river. A hole halfway up the bank has caught her attention and she inserts her muzzle well into it, taking several deep, snuffling breaths. She pauses and then backs out and starts to dig with abandon, flinging sand-colored dirt into a tapering mound as she enlarges the entrance of the hole. The male stands off to the side watching. In minutes her body is halfway in. He comes over to try to help but instead, gets showered with sand and dirt, and immediately lowers his ears, squints, and purses his lips as he takes the first spray of it in the face. He jumps to the side in quick order and shakes himself, content to watch as his mate disappears into the ground. She comes out some time later smelling of moist earth and peppered with sand. She shakes, and they trot off on their next mission.

She keeps this up over the next few weeks until half a dozen dens are established in various places around the territory. She is still restless, spending almost more time seeking holes than hunting voles, until one late afternoon when she smells the remnants of an old porcupine den in the rocks in a private place at the heart of one of the woodlots. The opening faces south and warmth lingers at the mouth of it, despite the weakening rays of the setting winter sun.

She scratches at the rock and moves the dried leaves around into a loose pile.

She lowers herself into the crevice and spins around into a tight ball, facing outward. The male comes over to check it out and gently stretches his nose toward her in an effort to gather in the smells of this new home. An unexpected snarl and nip cause him to jerk his head to the side and into the dirt, and in doing so he picks up several quills left by the former occupant. He jumps back away from the den and raises his front leg in an effort to sweep the quills from the right side of his muzzle, but they remain embedded.

After several minutes the sting begins to subside. The female is now curled into a tight ball, sleeping. The male gazes at the mouth of the den for a moment before rising to leave for the evening hunt.[4]

CHAPTER 10

A Short Story about a Small Moose

It may be the worst kind of anthropomorphism to characterize beavers as busy. They are no busier than a rattlesnake that lies motionless for days in the desert, waiting for prey. Both are equally conscientious, in their own ways, doing what needs to be done with the instincts and skills that have been bestowed on them to allow them to stay alive and reproduce. But it is the work of beavers and the similarity of their lifestyle to our own that make us think of them as particularly industrious and clever. They build stuff—intricate dams and cozy lodges—and they maintain and improve the structures they create. Over time they extend their reach by building longer and higher dams, which increase the size of the impoundments that flood the land, giving the beavers fresh access to the woody vegetation that they need to live. When it comes to real estate, people and beavers operate in many of the same ways. Maybe that is the simple reason that so many people have come to hate them so much.

I stand on the edge of one such large beaver impoundment this early spring morning. The last of the winter's ice, huddling along the dark edges of the wetland, hangs on to existence with thin, bony fingers. The full sun that will prevail this afternoon is likely to spell the end of winter's grip on this or any other marsh in the region. The air is full of the scents and sounds of early spring in southern New England: the rusty calls of red-winged blackbirds, the winnowing of snipe, the rich, musty smell of decaying vegetation mixed with marsh water. Although this is the middle of Massachusetts, it might as well be the center of some state in the Far West, given the feeling of solitude and the sense of open space that these wildlife management areas impart. I like the marshes; you can be alone here, in one of the most densely populated parts of the country.

Across the water I see two beavers hunched up on their hindquarters on shore. They gather small twigs to themselves with their dexterous front paws and nibble away at them; blueberry, I think, or maybe young dogwood. They are aware of my presence as they eat but at the moment are not concerned.

The beaver has undergone such a vast transformation in the American consciousness that it is hard to comprehend. Its incredible abundance made it an economic resource that gave rise to a nation, before it was extirpated nearly to the point of extinction. This species that we came so close to losing altogether has become another North American success story. We have been there and back again with the beaver. Now we stutter and fret over the renewed success and growing abundance of beavers. Today so many live in so many places that from the confines of our human perspective we consider them "overabundant."

I wish that I could come here in the fall when the pelts are prime and take a few, feed the cooked meat to my dogs, and clothe my family and friends in the luxurious fur, leaving most of the beavers to continue their life among us. I would rather do that than brand them as pests, go after them in the spring when their activities most conflict with our own, and deposit them like so much worthless biomass in the blighted creation of our modern landscape, the town dump.

The beavers are in the water now, and the bigger of the two swims over in stealth, looking a bit like an overweight torpedo. She cruises up alongside the bank where I sit, and with a whap of her large, flat tail she sends a spray of water and a message of ownership my way, directing me to leave. I smile and wish that it really did work that way for them . . . they'd slap the water, and we would simply move onto higher ground.

She slips down into the dark water. I decide that it would be a good thing to show her she can win one of these contests once in a while, so I wade across the shallows to the far bank, and I leave her be. 🌿

The call came in over Dave's cell phone just as we were pulling into the driveway after another morning of looking for moose. A young moose had been reported in a horse paddock in Holden. It had been hanging around for the past few days, and now it was in among the horses and might be injured. Could we come and help? We could, and in a moment Dave had the truck turned around and we were heading for Holden.

Massachusetts, like a lot of states, has a large-animal response team (LART). Here it comprises MassWildlife personnel and Environmental Police Officers (EPOs). One of their many duties is to deal with animals like moose, deer, and bears that wander into towns and other places where they can quickly get into trouble. The goal is to protect both animals and people, and when the animal isn't able to move out of the area on its own or with some persuasion from the LART, the response is to tranquilize it and relocate it to a more appropriate place—a state forest or wildlife management area, for example. Normally, relocating wildlife is a bad idea—it is also against the law—but this is an important exception. It is part of modern urban-suburban wildlife management.

We zipped along State Highway 122, out of New Salem and through Petersham, Barre, and Rutland. All nice towns, the homes and small farms intermixed with fields and woods edged with old stone walls and split-rail fences. Spring was coming on, and it was one of the first truly warm days after a long cold winter. The maples and oaks looked to be seriously considering opening their buds, as the sun soaked in like liniment on winter-weary muscles. On some of the farms black earth had been plowed smooth and horses shook themselves and let fly their winter coats. Chickens scratched up duff in the country lanes and people strolled along the town streets, enjoying the sunny day. It is Massachusetts as I know it and as I want it to remain.

The directions were good: we got to the farm and pulled into the muddy drive, where we were greeted by a couple of big dogs, straining their vocal cords and their leads as they vied for the attention of these strangers. Our focus was diverted as soon as we stepped out of the truck, though. The moose, a yearling female, stood quietly in the corner of the field in the shade of a single pine tree. The horses, a team of beautiful Shires, were confined to the barn. The young moose may have been seeking the company of like individuals, but the horses wanted nothing to do with this strange creature. They were edgy and nervous, and the owner thought one of them might have kicked the moose when she got too close.

The owner welcomed us and thanked us for coming, then filled us in on the story of this moose. She was still young enough that she should have been with her mother, but no one could recall seeing a cow moose in the vicinity for the past few months. The calf had wandered down from the surrounding wooded hills and onto the horse farm several times in the past month or two, but this was the first time she had gotten through the fence and into the paddock.

We discussed the situation with the MassWildlife folks, and it was decided that we would dart the moose, haul her up the road a piece to some state land, and release her there. So we loaded up the dart gun, and Dave walked the fence line to about twenty yards from the moose, then launched a dart into her rump.

She collapsed pretty quickly, and in minutes the farmer's young daughter had revved up their tractor and driven over to us. We rolled the moose—small but still heavy—into the bucket, and the daughter threw the gears into reverse. We ran to keep up, holding the moose's head and limbs up off the ground as best we could. We loaded her into the back of our open pickup truck and headed out.

The gate was locked on our first choice of a release area. We decided we would have to go up the road a bit and unload the animal there, in a meadow surrounded by state-owned forest. The release site was just off the road, so when the moose came to we would have to herd her into the woods and away from the traffic, light though it was in this area.

We reached the spot and backed the truck in as far as we could. A thin layer of snow still covered everything. It was about two o'clock in the afternoon when we slid the animal from the bed onto the ground. We put a GPS collar around the neck of the moose and small plastic tags in her ears and then gave her a shot of the antidote—the drug that speeds the reversal of the tranquilizing agent and puts the animal back on its feet sooner. Then we stood back and waited.

Cars trickled by on this country road, and soon a few people stopped and asked about the moose. "Was it hit by a car?" was the most common question. "Did someone shoot it?" people asked a few times. We took turns walking up to the car window and telling the story. Everyone was interested, and everyone was relieved to know that the moose was not hurt.

In a while, more people came by, and now they were getting out of their cars. Mothers brought their kids over to us and asked politely if they could pet the moose. We would say, "Normally you should never do that, but you can come up and take a closer look." The kids were mostly quiet and their faces were all awe and curiosity, eyes wide as full moons. One mom loaded up her kids after they got a good look; she started off but backed up and got out again, standing by the door on the driver's side, waving a can.

"Say, I was thinking," she says, "Is the moose hungry? Would it like some peanuts?"

We laugh and thank her. She may be a bit hungry, but she eats buds and tree bark, we tell her. The woman laughs and waves good-bye as she gets back into her car and drives away.

By then, we are growing a bit nervous. The moose is not coming out from under the drug the way she should. Outside it is still light and warm, but we look up and see that the day is waning. We quietly discuss matters and decide to try a bit more of the antidote. In the meantime, traffic is backing up. People are stopped, and the police have shown up. The moose is lying there quietly. Her head is up but she is showing no desire to leave the area.

We find out from the police that the word has gotten out over the radio that there is a moose down on Sterling Road, and the whole town of Holden is turning out to get a look. People are curious, interested, and polite, but the mood is building to almost a party atmosphere. "What else is there to do in Holden?" we hear someone say. We are starting to recognize some of the vehicles, several of which have been back two or three times.

Eventually, enough time has elapsed, probably about two hours or more, that people start to leave. Several of them turn, as they regain their cars, to thank us. "Thanks for taking care of the moose," they say; they smile and wave and move on. They are really appreciative, sincere in their interest and concern for this animal and even for us. In a profession often assailed by critique and criticism from all quarters the appreciation makes us feel pretty good.

Other cars are still showing up, but as the daylight fades, fewer and fewer people remain on the scene. By dusk, Dave, Andrew, and I are the only ones left, and we are worried and a bit confused about this moose. Is she sick? Was she hurt worse than we thought? Did we give her too much of the drug to begin with? We decide we'd better take the

GPS collar off because although such a collar is no problem for a moose, even one this young, we don't want to be receiving data from an animal that may have an injury or a sickness of which we are not aware.

It is dark now, and we're still waiting. Occasionally one of us gets out of the truck and checks on the moose, but she is still lying in the snow with her head up, having apparently decided that this is where she will stay for the night. Normally we would have agreed to let the animal be and checked in on her in the morning, but she is too close to the road to leave now. It's the worry I'm feeling, more than the time of evening or the cold, that is making me grouchy.

For the third time today the same light gray SUV pulls up in front of us.

"What the hell do these people want now?" I say, half kidding but a little irritated, expecting criticism and unanswerable questions, worried as I am about the little moose and our public exposure. "Don't they have anything better to do today?"

A pretty, middle-aged woman gets out of the driver's seat and walks over to our vehicle. Dave rolls down the window.

"You boys looked so cold and you've been here so long, I thought you might like some hot chocolate," she says. "And I brought you some homemade cookies."

Dave and Andrew give me simultaneous sidelong glances. I smile sheepishly.

"Well, that is really nice of you," says Dave, always the gentleman, turning back to the woman. "We were getting a little hungry. Didn't expect to be out here this long."

She passes in a full thermos and a large Ziploc bag packed with chocolate chip cookies, still warm. She even has paper cups and napkins for us. We all thank her profusely and she asks that we just put the thermos in her mailbox when we are done. She describes her place just up the road.

"Good luck, and thanks for taking care of the moose," she says, in ever-so-pleasant a way.

We pass the hot drinks and cookies all round. I think maybe I don't deserve any, but I take my share anyway. Dave and Andrew drink their cocoa and eat their cookies, feigning interest in something outside, as they look out the windows, trying to hide the smirks on their faces.

"All right, I'm a jerk," I finally blurt out.

"We weren't going to say anything," they laugh, and I smile and take another bite of a cookie.

Time passes slowly; still the moose does not move. The MassWildlife folks return, and we decide it is time for the animal to get to her feet, so we roust her up. Then, after a few false starts, we actually walk her across the field and back into the woods to a place where she is safe from the road, at least in the short term. A stand of young white pines growing close together blocks the wind, and there is browse around for her in the morning. We feel much better about leaving the moose here, so we whisper some words of encouragement and leave the little animal on her own for the night. The last thing we do before hitting the road toward home is to stop by the woman's house and leave the thermos and a thank-you note in her mailbox.

The following morning Bill Davis of MassWildlife checks on the moose and reports that she is still in the area and up and moving about, and he sees evidence that the animal has been eating some buds. All that is good news, yet I wonder what is to become of this young moose. I also think about how the townspeople responded, their kindness and interest and genuine concern for the moose and for us. When it comes right down to it, people really do love and appreciate wildlife. It is a lesson that I have learned in the past, and only my own pigheadedness and occasional bouts with misanthropy make it necessary for me to learn it again and again. But I am convinced that love of nature is as inherent in us as the struggle to survive, the desire to prosper, the urge to protect our children, or the motivation to help a neighbor in need. The feelings for the wild are there, buried under the layers of designer clothing or the latest in outdoor wear and the psychological shields we all use to protect ourselves. We need only to find how to tap into it and make it part of our national character, and a true motivation behind our choices and actions, before what we do have—and love—is gone forever.

The male coyote trots into view carrying a squirrel. He deposits it at the mouth of the den and lowers his head just enough to see past the rim of rock and into the dark cavity. He waits for the female, who is usually fairly prompt in retrieving the kill, but she does not appear this morning.

From deep inside the den he hears the sound of a thin, quiet cry, barely audible. He can tell the female is licking something; she keeps it up at a constant rate: the licking goes on as if it will never stop. As his eyes adjust to the darkness, he makes out the forms of a number of small, dark pups. One is squirming as the female goes on with her persistent attention. The rest are nuzzled up tight against her belly, quiet except for the slightest of suckling sounds. He stares in for quite a while and then turns to lie just outside the den, to begin his vigil.[1]

CHAPTER 11

Coyote Spirits

I called my first border collie Kit because of her ears. I was working on kit foxes in the Great Basin desert of southeastern Oregon when I got her. Kit was a black-and-white short-haired border collie and she had big, pricked-up ears, like a kit fox. She was a character, like all border collies, and a good companion, like all border collies. We went everywhere together. On one of those days, during the days when we were always together, we were walking a transect through the sagebrush southwest of Burns Junction, looking for evidence that kit foxes still occupied this remote corner of Oregon.

The morning was crystal clear and cool: a morning made for walking. I followed my compass line, looking for fox sign, while Kit circled around and smelled everything as if she were on a mission to account for every jackrabbit and kangaroo rat in the county. The sun was just up, and it cast a shine on the vegetation, the unfiltered light outlining every leaf and stem in perfect clarity, the modest warmth filling the air with that sweet smell of sage. Meadowlarks sent their calls bubbling forth to mark the start of the day, and a lone mustang whinnied somewhere way to the north. Far behind me on the two-lane road, I could hear the distant revving of a truck engine as the driver progressed through an endless series of gears. He was traveling by Burns Junction on his way south to Winnemucca, without even any notion of stopping, but in his passing he became for a moment the closest human being to me for several miles.

It is big, open country, lonely country, out there on those sagebrush flats, and so when you are not alone, you notice. Not long after Kit and I started walking, I knew we were being followed. It was one of those moments when you instinctively look over your shoulder, without knowing why. To my right and just behind was a coyote, its face bright and tawny in the full glow of the rising sun, peering at us over the top of the sagebrush. There was another coyote to my left. And as these two disappeared into the vegetation, I looked behind to see a third, and ahead a fourth. I called to Kit, checked the compass, and continued.

For what seemed like the next half hour, eyes appeared at various spots right above the brush, as the coyotes watched and followed, followed and watched. I am guessing there were four of them—could have been two or five. It was hard to count and hard to say as they alternately appeared and disappeared, their stares always fixed in our direction.

It was fascinating and a bit eerie. They kept a close eye on me, but they were drawn to Kit and watched her with a constant curiosity. They maintained their mobile vigil until the sun came farther up into the sky to warm the earth, and then they vaporized and were gone like the early morning moisture.

Wildlife biologists and those like them are sometimes accused of liking animals more than people. It is not entirely true. I like people. I have been blessed with a wonderful family—on both sides—and my friendships are precious to me, even though I have become terrible at corresponding with (and even worse at telephoning) old friends who live far away. I mark the successes in my life in large part by time spent with my family and by the friends I have had and the company I have kept. I often long for a life of solitude amid many square miles of wild land, but I am not so naive as to think that I could be happy without lots of people in my life. As much as I enjoy time alone, I also get lonely, and sometimes feelings of loneliness stay with me like a lingering cold.

Too often, though, people disappoint me. I have been told by past girlfriends, a former wife, and my current wife that I expect too much of people. A supervisor sat me down one day and explained that if I anticipate certain responses from people, I will always be frustrated. I know I can be too demanding in my relationships. I think I can be a good friend and partner, but a difficult one at times, and my behavior can wear us all down. I know I have a temper, born of keeping stuff inside until I can no longer contain it; then at some unforeseen moment a small, unrelated event causes an eruption, like a sneeze starting an avalanche.

Like most people, I am prone to periods of minor depression, although on most days I am pretty content, so over the years my life has been a series of highs punctuated by occasional lows. I have seen therapists once or twice in the past, have read a dozen or so books on improving my outlook and controlling my anger, and—God help me— have even sat through a few seminars where they make you stand up and bare your soul or, worse yet, playact, in front of a roomful of strangers.

I have given all that up now. I actually prefer the mood swings. I know I am mostly a happy person, but every so often I almost need the low moods and the anger and frustration. I don't really know why. That's life, I suppose. Don't you want from time to time to step out into the world and raise some hell—just start swinging at whatever comes by? Doesn't all of this—all of us—just get to you once in a while? When I was very young, I used to think I was the only one to feel this way. Now I realize that most people are like this. It is not so much the bouts of frustration and anger that we sometimes feel but the desire to rebel, to go against the flow, to succeed despite the opposition that the world can throw our way. It must be the coyote in us.

It *is* a predator's sort of life. For the most part you get along with the world around you. You loll in the meadow with the sun on your belly, wade in the stream, sniff at the pine boughs. You tussle with your youngsters and nuzzle your mate. You stroll through the forest and feel the soft push of leaf duff on the pads of your feet. And then, sudden as the slap on the bottom that forced the first breath of life into your lungs, the recognition hits you that it is time to go out on the hunt. The adrenaline rushes in, and the blood flows into your limbs. Your eyes narrow and your breathing deepens. You are keenly aware of the world around you. You spring into action, in the knowledge that nothing can stop you, and it all goes fast and right. You know you are alive, and if you want to stay that way, you know you need to make a move.

The same is true for prey species. They live a docile life, filling their bellies with plants and ruminating on the ways of nature; but as soon as these animals sense pursuit, they are off and running. Get too close and you may incur a hoof in the teeth, an antler in the side, a vicious bite, a deep scratch, or a mouthful of poison, a mortal wound of some kind. We humans were both predator and prey once, a long, long time ago, and once we not only understood this—we lived it. Nowadays we unwittingly find other ways, other outlets, to express this identity that we still harbor deep inside.

Such meandering thoughts occupy my mind as I proceed west on Route 2 along the Millers River. I am on my way to work, the summer day upon me as I drive along with the flow of the river. I am in a bit of a mood, so I've decided to go a different way to the office today. It is longer, with more traffic; in fact, it makes no sense at all to take this route, which is why I am doing it.

Lost in thought, I've just rounded a bend in the highway when I see a large carcass way up ahead in the middle of the road. I first think it is a dead dog, mowed down by traffic after running loose from one of the nearby farms. But I soon see that I am wrong. The animal lifts its head and struggles to eye the oncoming traffic. A small streak of horror rushes down the back of my neck. The animal is hit but not yet dead, its body twisted and partially crushed. It cannot get up and run away into the hills. It is injured beyond recovery, I know: the end is near but not yet here. The only movement the poor thing can manage is to raise its head a few inches for a moment in a feeble gesture before dropping it back onto the unforgiving pavement. I see then that this is not a dog. It is an adult coyote.

I jerk the wheel, pull over onto a wide spot on the shoulder, and get out of the truck. The coyote lifts its head in an attempt to see me, and again that action sends a sick feeling of pity and helplessness through me. I stand there with my hands on my hips for a moment, wondering what to do. Traffic whizzes by, barely slowing down, if at all, and people eye me as they fly past. I imagine they think I hit the "dog," but probably they have no idea what's going on. My only thought is that I want to put this poor animal out of its misery and end its pain and indignity now.

I am reluctant to drag it off to the side of the road, for fear that that may worsen its suffering. Besides, that would not put an end to its distress, only intensify and prolong it. I look back at my truck. The only thing I can think of at the moment is to drive over it and finish the act. I am pretty sure I have nothing in the back to help me, but I look anyway. There lies a heavy flat-bladed shovel that I happened to throw in the truck bed yesterday after doing some work in the yard. I grab it and roll up a sleeve.

I am marching out into the road only partially aware of the streaming traffic. It is only a few steps, but it feels like a long way. It occurs to me that these people driving by must think I am a madman, but at the moment I don't give a good goddamn what they think. I am only concerned with this animal, and that it suffer no longer.

I reach the coyote and without hesitation swing the shovel down flat on the side of its head. And then I do it again, and again, three or four times in all. Its skull is crushed and the life is gone. I reel a bit and step back, but I make myself stop. I am not finished. I refuse to leave it lying in the middle of the road like some piece of trash when an endless procession of cars is speeding by on either side.

When there is a break in the traffic, I pull the carcass over to the shoulder on the other side of my truck, hiding us both from the prying eyes of the passersby. I squat down and look carefully at the coyote. Despite my vigorous swings of the shovel, its head is not completely misshapen. It is still handsome as it lies there in death. I notice a few porcupine quills in its muzzle. At first I think that maybe the pain or irritation caused it to run out into the road, but I doubt it. They are probably just the traces of its former life as a predator.

I stay for a while. I am not hearing any traffic. The world is not quiet—I am just not hearing it. The coyote and I are quiet together. Everything is still, and the color has gone out of my surroundings. The rancher and writer Dayton Hyde spoke of a coyote friend of his that he came upon moments after it had died. He wrote the most beautiful lines I have ever read by someone who has witnessed the death of an animal: "A light breeze stroked his lush fall coat as though the hands of spirits were already there to stroke and comfort him."[1]

But on that day I neither saw nor felt comfort at the hands of spirits. In fact, I felt that no such spirits at all remained in the state of Massachusetts. They had been driven out by the overwhelming presence of people and roads and traffic and houses and malls and cell phones and laptops. We had traded their presence for our bustling lifestyles, an endless array of gadgets and consumer goods, and the empty promise of more money as the way to fulfillment. We had forced their departure, and they had up and left without our noticing. They had moved away some time ago, someplace far away, where the crush of humanity had not yet created a place where there was little tolerance for coyotes or creatures like them and the spirits that might protect and comfort them.

I drove the rest of the way to work slowly, bound and determined to keep to the speed limit no matter how long the line of traffic behind me got. On that day at that time and on that road, no more coyotes, or turtles or birds or snakes or chipmunks or woodchucks, would be killed.

I avoided people for the remainder of the day. That night I gave the dogs a little extra food and took them for a longer walk.

🐾 In a grassy field in Massachusetts, in the shadows formed by the late-afternoon sun and a small grove of trees, a coyote lies with her head up. The light, mixing with the colors of her coat as she straddles the shadow line, blends her into the landscape and gives her the privacy she is looking for in a world busy with people. She is relaxed but ever watchful, and she takes in her surroundings with her every breath.

Some movement in the grass just in front of her has her full attention: she stares at the spot, ears up, eyes forward. She is well aware of what is in there but watches intently anyway. Seconds later, in a tiny explosion of light-brown fur, a pup tumbles out of the tall vegetation and bounds toward her, reaching her with a final awkward lunge. She tilts her head up as he licks her lips and muzzle with unbridled enthusiasm. Four more youngsters stumble out of the grass and tussle all around her, wrestling among themselves with open mouths and gangly legs, and all is mayhem as they roll and scrape and nip and pounce, bouncing off Mom as they tear into one another in raucous play. The female takes the abuse with all the patience of motherhood and watches her offspring as she watches the world all around her.

🐾 She has been called "ky-ote" and "ky-o-tee"—coyotl, cayeutes, cojote, and *Canis latrans*. Some have referred to her as song dog or prairie tenor, bur-

rowing dog, brush wolf, prairie wolf, cased wolf, or barking wolf.[2] A ghost of the plains of a century past, a ghost of our cities in more modern times.

She has been accused of being a varmint, a scourge, a pest, and a weed, and she has been praised as an icon of the American West, elevated to a key role as a top carnivore in the balance of nature, and deified as God's dog.

She is a dedicated mother and an excellent hunter, a long-distance traveler and a tireless scavenger. She is a carnivore and an omnivore and a vegetarian, depending on circumstances and opportunities. She is recognized by her track and scat, her voice and her scent. She is known for her cunning, her slyness, and her ability to survive and persist and move and spread. She has taken up residence in virtually every ecological community and human environment on the continent and has eaten everything humankind and nature have to offer. She is among the most adaptable of species.

She has befriended badgers and mated with dogs and wolves.[3] She is strangely familiar and altogether foreign. She has survived decades of cyanide, strychnine, and 1080; .222s and .308s and 30-aught-6s; steel-jawed traps and wire snares; barbed-wire fences and speeding vehicles; bad press, half-truths, and outright lies.[4]

She has found her way into the stories and songs and poetry and legends of all who have ever shared this land with her. We have used her name and image for our business and sports team logos while we have hung her carcass on our fences and tacked her hide to our sheds. We have worn her fur and put a bounty on her body and shared some of our most memorable evenings with her serenades and songs. We praise her and idolize her, and fear her and hate her, sometimes all in the same breath, and as such she has become an analogy for our relationship with all of nature. We have lived with her for our entire existence in North America, and if we were to lose her altogether, we would forever be missing a piece of what it is to be American.

But there is little chance of that, because she is a coyote and she knows how to get by.

CHAPTER 12

A Suburban Land Ethic

It is difficult to think about giving up the fieldwork, although there is a constant pull to do so. Life and work are too busy; I am no longer at the age or stage in life and my career where fieldwork is essential. I know I could advance further and faster if I spent more time in the office, in front of the computer—analyzing, synthesizing, writing. Data collection in the field is largely what the graduate students and field techs do. I administer, oversee, and supervise the research now, and I should be attending to business: bringing in more grant money, serving on more committees, and spending more time hobnobbing with colleagues at meetings. I should be doing a better job of staying up on the literature and the recent advancements in computer technology. Most of all, I should be writing and publishing more papers: papers on primary research, papers that synthesize other research, papers that will be cited by other researchers much more than the handful of times my current papers ever are. I should be the lead author on several, coauthor on many, and sole author of a few. I should be producing journal articles and books and book chapters and edited works. My productivity should be consistent and constant, like water over a wheel in a millpond. I should put out at least three papers a year—four or five a year would be better—and several of them in the higher-tier journals, where the competition for space is fierce and the peer-review process brutal. I have been told I need to do this to reach the next rung on the ladder. I stand on that ladder now and sway in the wind: as I look up, the distance grows greater with every step. The hayloft door is open at the top, but I am not really sure what is in there—something good, they say.

Despite such occasional misgivings about personal job performance and the bouts of drudgery that accompany all jobs, being a research biologist is good work, satisfying work, work that allows for creativity and accomplishment. There is an excitement to analyzing data and seeing the results after the long process of collection, and a thrill at getting that letter of acceptance for one of your manuscripts from the editor of a journal. You have a sense of fulfillment in guiding dedicated students, contributing in even a small way to the science of a subject, and helping the hardworking managers who toil on the front lines of wildlife biology day in and day out.

But fieldwork is why most of us got into this business. We like being outdoors and working with animals. Fieldwork is time-consuming, though. A day spent in the field is a day spent away from all the other things that go into being a professional wildlife biologist. Fieldwork does help me stay in shape some, but it also wears me down. I am tired after being out for two days, so the two days away from the office translate into another day of slow-motion activity and half-hearted taps at the keyboard. I struggle to catch up and make progress. As always, the paperwork never ends and the e-mail never stops.

Yet it is difficult to think about giving up the fieldwork. I wake to another fine spring day. Leaf-out is fully under way, and the hermit and wood thrushes outside the window are calling, leaving me to wonder why I am dallying. It comes as no surprise that I give in to the day and heed the advice of the thrushes. An hour later I am in a small boat motoring across quiet water into the territory of a pair of common loons.

If there is a cliché in nature, it is the common loon—mysterious bird of mist-covered lakes, harbinger of spring breakup and annual rebirth, wilderness icon of the north. Clichés such as these are no mere trifles of the unimaginative mind, but rather a testament to the power and universality of the symbol itself. Common loons reach people in ways that link us all in an innate love and respect of nature. For some, for those of us who cannot live without wild things, as Leopold said, the feelings come easy.[1] In others of us, for whatever reason, the feelings may be suppressed; but they are there. For you it may be the bugle of an elk on the slopes of the Rocky Mountains, the movement of pronghorn across an open plain, butterflies in a meadow, a cardinal perched on a tree limb in the garden, or the incessant chipping calls of spring peepers in the evening. It could simply be a nice sunset or the feel and scent of the summer sea breeze as you walk across sand dunes. Whatever it is, it is something that often lies still and deep, like these quiet Quabbin waters.

Nature, in the form of the common loon, brings these feelings to the surface and connects us in some way to the natural world, our world. For city dweller and farmer, logger and environmentalist, hunter and antihunter, politician and activist, office worker and ranchhand, Easterner and Westerner, it is images like the common loon that make us pause in our suspicions of one another's motives, and for a moment we may respect one another and grasp, in some small way, our place in the world.

Now I watch through my scope and dutifully record, every sixty seconds, a two-letter code that represents a behavior of the loon on her nest at the moment I happen to be watching. As the data sheet fills, I learn a bit more about loons, in both a scientific and a personal way, one minute at a time. At the end of one hundred minutes the data sheet is full and I have a record of a tiny fraction of the life of a loon.

Now it is time for me to move on. I start up the engine and slowly swing the boat out of the cove, looking back to catch one more glimpse of the loon as she continues to attend to her eggs.

It is a summer evening like many other summer evenings . . . pleasant, still, warm, but not too warm. I am home from work. It was a good day, but I am ready to relax and take it easy for a spell. Ki's mother, Myrtle, has been staying with us, and we decide to have supper out on the screened-in porch, where we can take the air without having to deal with the mosquitoes. Ki prepares the food, and Myrtle and I bring one item after another out to the wrought-iron table. Soon we are all sitting down to eat, the dogs stretched out at our feet on the cool porch boards. They'll be up in a few minutes to sniff around for any small bits of food that might make it to the floor. The chickens are out nipping at the blades of grass on the front lawn. We have eight of them right now, although the number tends to vary. We have found that eight will yield more than enough eggs for ourselves with plenty left over to give to family and friends. Through the trees we can hear the neighbor kid playing out in his yard, and the chirps and calls of a few birds, but it is otherwise quiet.

Soon that peace is shattered by an alarm sounded by all eight chickens in unison. They are squawking loudly, running for all they are worth across the lawn and back toward the porch, bouncing from one leg to the other and holding their wings out as they make for cover. Something has got them going. From the adjacent woods and around the big spruce near the driveway a young coyote loops into the yard, at full tilt. He races right toward the porch. Ki is already up and heading for the door, yelling at him to get away, as if that might work. The dogs haven't even realized yet that anything is amiss: they lift their heads off the floor to see what all the ruckus is for. Myrtle, not being able to see too well, asks what all the fuss is about. I sit and watch the action, taking another bite out of my chicken leg.

"Looks like a coyote decided to invite himself to dinner, Myrt," I say.

The coyote makes a swing toward the house and, not three feet below us, grabs one of our biggest and slowest Dominiques in his mouth and attempts to carry her off. But she proves to be too big a mouthful, and that, plus Ki jumping off the porch, causes him to drop the hen and head back for the spruce. As he does, he deftly reaches out to the side and grabs one of the younger birds, a cinnamon-colored Araucana. The coyote doesn't slow down for a moment, and in a flash he has disappeared past the big tree and back into the forest, as quickly as he appeared. Just like that, everything's over and it is quiet again, save for the nervous clucks of the surviving chickens as they mill about the porch. We check the big Dominique. She looks none the worse for wear, except for a dull, glazed look in her eyes. Still in shock, I'm sure.

We try to follow his trail into the woods, looking for light-brown chicken feathers or some other sign of what just happened, but we find nothing. Ki is a bit distressed. The dogs have their hackles up and are retracing the crime. I stare off into the woods, straining for a glimpse of the coyote but knowing all I will see is empty forest.

I crane my neck to see farther into the trees. "Bold little bastard," I whisper, to no one in particular, but I am smiling. He used our foot trail to enter and leave the yard, but then I imagine he kept to the woods, skirting the neighboring field, heading off down the slope, never stopping until he had reached safe ground. That's what I'd do. I'm sure the chicken was dead before he stopped to examine his prize.

I direct one last searching glance toward the woods before heading back to the house and going in through the kitchen door.

One thing coyotes teach us is that like it or not, we share the land with others. Of course, not just with coyotes—we share the land with our families and neighbors, with the people who have come before us and with those who will come after. We also share the land with every other form of life that inhabits this earth: every insect and plant, every fish, fowl, mammal, reptile, and amphibian, all the invertebrates, the named and nameless fungi and lichens, and the legions of molds and bacteria and viruses. The others—those we share the land with—need the land just as much as we do. What's more, we need them, no matter how we try to convince ourselves that we can go it alone. Our continued existence is predicated on sharing the land, whether we acknowledge that or not. We are sometimes cavalier in our judgments, occasionally complacent in our valuations, and all-too-often insensitive in wielding the power we hold over the earth. We can be unthinking and egocentric—yet we are not beyond learning. What we lack—and some who went before us have tried to make us understand this—is a philosophy, a code, or an ethic, to help us step up to our responsibility of conservation and assume our birthright of stewardship. We have the knowledge, the capability, and the wherewithal to do so—all we need is the will and the guidance.

Of the many who have spoken of our need for such a code, perhaps none was more eloquent or persuasive than Aldo Leopold. Aldo Leopold was a scientist, conservationist, and writer. He has been credited with being one of the founders of the conservation movement and the father of modern wildlife management. Among his many accomplishments was *A Sand County Almanac,* the book published posthumously in 1949. Leopold had died the year before of a heart attack while he was helping a neighbor put out a grass fire. *A Sand County Almanac* is basically a series of essays on wildlife, ecology, people's role in nature, and the land, which are organized in part around the calendar year and the seasons and focused on Leopold's small farm in central Wisconsin. It is arguably Leopold's greatest work and most lasting contribution. One of the last pieces in the collection, "The Land Ethic," may be the most important in a book full of important essays. In it Leopold states, "All ethics so far evolved rest upon a single premise: that the individual is a member of a community of interdependent parts. His instincts prompt him to compete for his place in that community, but his ethics prompt him also to cooperate (perhaps in order that there may be a place to compete for)." He goes on to explain, "The land ethic simply enlarges the boundaries of the community to include soils, water, plants, and animals, or collectively: the land."[2]

We are members of that community of the land. You may not feel it if you live in the middle of a large city or a sprawling suburb, or you may think it is applicable only to those who farm or ranch or otherwise make their living directly from the land, but the truth is that we all do—we all make our living off the land. No matter where or how you live, your livelihood, health, and well-being are based on the land. Your water, food, air, basic necessities and material possessions, recreational opportunities and vacations, and in short everything that you depend on for survival and a good and decent life depend on the land—and that is true whether you live in a cabin in the wilderness, a small community in farming country, a high-rise condominium in the city, or a house in the suburbs.

We have been rich in land in this country for our entire history to date, but that hallmark is changing before our eyes. Land, and all the things it does and provides, are becoming increasingly scarce under our regimen of development and sprawl. Land use cannot necessarily be measured directly in acres—that is, the number of acres that are built up versus the number that are not. The way we use and view the land involves much more than the physical manifestations of the built environment. The important thing is the quantity of resources we demand and consume, because all of them ultimately come from one place . . . the land.

In "The Land Ethic" Leopold laments our attitude toward our resources: soil, "which we are sending helter-skelter downriver"; waterways, "which we assume have no function except to turn turbines, float barges, and carry off sewage"; plants, "of which we exterminate whole communities without batting an eye"; and animals, "of which we have extirpated many of the largest and most beautiful of species."[3] Certainly we have made some progress toward turning the tide in our approach to the destruction of all these aspects of the ecological community. Still, we must ask ourselves, Are we really doing anything different than we did close to a hundred years ago? Are we as good citizens as we might be in our ecological community?

Leopold makes some of his most compelling statements about land in the foreword to *A Sand County Almanac*—for example, "We abuse land because we regard it as a commodity belonging to us. When we see land as a community to which we belong, we may begin to use it with love and respect."[4] Here he is not talking about never using the land. Leopold was a hunter and forester as well as a conservationist. He believed in harvesting things from the land for human use. He lived a privileged and comfortable life as a university professor. Yet he believed that it was possible to husband resources with care and respect for the land and for the products of the land, whether trees or vegetables, wildlife or livestock, water or minerals.

He defined the ideal approach to land in both ecology and ethics: "That land is a community is the basic concept of ecology, but that land is to be loved and respected is an extension of ethics." Thus, to Leopold's mind, the human endeavors of science and ethics, the objective and the subjective, the pragmatic and empirical, not to mention the ethereal and metaphysical, all contributed to a philosophy that would not only help us survive and live well, but also lighten our tread on the foundation that supports us in every aspect of life. Leopold realized that not everyone would see it the same way he did; indeed, he was very much conscious of the American obsession with material wealth, even back in the 1930s and '40s: "Such a view of land and people is, of course, subject to the blurs and distortions of personal experience and personal bias. But wherever the truth may lie, this much is crystal-clear: our bigger-and-better society is now like a hypochondriac, so obsessed with its own economic health as to have lost the capacity to remain healthy. . . . Nothing could be more salutary at this stage than a little healthy contempt for a plethora of material blessings."[5]

A big part of our continuing problem is that we place *ownership* of the land above all else. I am not advocating a reduction in landowners' rights. Rather, I am pleading for an increased awareness of landowners' responsibilities. Again, I come back to Leopold, who wrote: "The land-relation is still strictly economic, entailing privileges but not obligations."

He suggested that we start by changing our perspective: "A land ethic changes the role of *Homo sapiens* from conqueror of the land-community to plain member and citizen of it." This was a change that he believed was "an evolutionary possibility and an ecological necessity."[6]

More than sixty years ago, Leopold attempted to move us into a new phase of conservation in the United States, the land ethic phase. That, I believe, is where we should focus much of our thought and energy and effort. Over the centuries people have developed a wide variety of ethical codes that deal with relations among individuals, and relations between individuals and society. According to Leopold, though, during the first half of the twentieth century we had yet to develop an ethic toward the land. We have made strides in that direction in the decades since the initial publication of *A Sand County Almanac,* but our development—and more important, our implementation—of a land ethic is not as far along as it should be at the outset of the twenty-first century.

We lag behind for a fundamental reason: we view land principally as property and believe we can do with it as we please, provided we possess a deed—a piece of paper—that says we own the acreage. Legal ownership entitles us to many privileges, but only indirectly implies any responsibilities. Rather than view ourselves as true members of a community—both human and ecological—we continue to view the land merely as "property" and ourselves merely as "individuals." This perception explains how some people can stand up at a town meeting and declare that their property is theirs to do with as they like, and they don't want anyone telling them what they can or cannot do. The alternative is to stand up and say something more along these lines: My property is indeed my property, and I have certain rights and privileges, but as the current custodian of that property I also have certain responsibilities and obligations.

The call for instituting a land ethic in our society is based on a simple premise: as long as we view land solely as property that we can use any way we wish, regardless of the consequences to the larger human and ecological communities to which we belong, we will continue to apportion, exploit, and exhaust the land that is left. The consequences of those actions are no longer avoidable. A change in thinking—some scientists call it a paradigm shift—is urgently needed, to ensure our livelihoods, protect our way of life, and pass on a secure future to our children, our grandchildren, and their children. We are products of the land. If we are conscious of all that the land provides and its importance to us, if we are protective of that, as we are of our families and our homes, a land ethic will become a natural part of our code for daily living. We will make respect for our land a part of our lifestyle.[7]

It is time to redefine progress. Progress used to be measured by the degree of development and economic growth we could show. That, and that alone, was our measure of the advancement of our society. We now need to define progress by the strides we have made toward living a more sustainable existence on earth, by consuming less and by adopting a land ethic.

The signs are hopeful, in the midst of a general atmosphere of worry. War, poverty, climate change, rising energy costs, failing economies, a failed health care system, record housing foreclosures . . . all of these create a backdrop of uneasiness and concern, as well they should. Amid all of this clamor, among all these claims on our attention, is a growing recognition of the need for us to accept the obvious and to do something about the plight of our environment.

Grassroots efforts offer one of the most hopeful signs of progress. Almost every town in Massachusetts, and in other states all around the country, is struggling to make development and growth more environmentally friendly. Ideas such as the creation of conservation subdivisions are being examined, debated, and adopted by more and more towns.[8] Reusing, reducing, and recycling have become more than just a catchy slogan: they are now routine in most places. In just that way, other habits change and the new habits become second nature. Local conservation trusts and land trusts are working with communities, developers, and town and city planning boards to set aside land, not only for conservation, but for farming, forestry, recreation, wildlife, and just plain old open space—to provide breathing room for a society that needs to stop and take a breath. Ordinary citizens are doing extraordinary things to save open space and set aside nature preserves, while at the same time allowing for development. It is very encouraging to see these groups at work, and it is inspiring to see the progress they are making.

As we go about redefining the word "progress," we also need to take back the word "environmentalism." Caring for the environment touches everyone. We can descend into our petty little political arguments and use "environmentalist" as a dirty word, but it does no one any good, including our kids and grandkids—in fact, especially them. We will never all agree about the best way to conduct our lives on this earth, but we can come to some agreement about the best way to treat the resources that sustain us and the land that produces those resources. We no longer have the luxury of resorting to factional bickering and meaningless sound bites. And those who think they own the word "environmentalism" need to broaden their perspective and wise up. Americans who hunt, fish, trap, log, ranch, and build are not the enemy; among them are good, caring, environmentally conscious people. When we alienate large groups of people because of our own biases, we do the environment and society not a lick of good. If we all band together in this new atmosphere of hope and change, there is no telling what we can accomplish.

🐾 It is late fall, and a few flakes swirl in the air. That hint of the first snow of the season is too much for me to bear. I need to be out in it. Stuffing the half-finished report into my briefcase, I abandon the office. I may look at that paper tonight, or more likely when I get up early tomorrow. I leave a recording on my answering machine: I am in the field for the rest of the day. . . . Leave a message . . . I will get back to you tomorrow. Thinking no one will notice, I quietly make my way down the back stairway. There are some things in the field I need to check on, anyway.

I take the back roads out of town, looping around the south end of the Quabbin and continuing eastward, heading for a spot where we have done both beaver and moose research. I'm thinking I'll check out this site for any moose activity. It would be nice to get a collar on an animal there. If I see

enough sign, I can report it to Dave and Ken. The driving is good; the roads are quiet, and there is virtually no traffic.

I drive along, watching the weather and the rural scenery—letting my mind roam. Something about this time of year always sets me to thinking, especially when I am driving or hiking around. It's the dichotomy: it is chilly and kind of gray and gloomy, yet beautiful, quiet and peaceful. It has the feel of the year's closing down, yet the world seems to open up. You can see far into the forest and the view of the sky is virtually unimpeded now that all the herbaceous growth is gone and the leaves are down.

Wisps of snow are just starting to blow across the road, and some of it is beginning to accumulate on the frozen ground. A dull light glints off of the tree limbs, and the farm fields lie fallow, the bare dirt turning to iron in the cold. The holiday season is approaching, and people have decorated their houses and yards with tiny lights to ward off the dark of the coming long, long winter nights.

I drive, thinking about some of the same old things. I am fully ensconced in my midfifties now and wondering how I got here so fast. I reminisce about the things I've done and the places I've been, at the same time realizing all the things I will never get to do and the places I will never get to see. I am not feeling sorry for myself over this—not really—but I do think of it more often now. I still have time, though—not for all of it, but for some of it. I have lived here in central Massachusetts longer than anywhere else in my adult life. In a lifetime of moving around I have always been searching for home, and I always thought that home was New England. And maybe it is. But I think I've got at least one more move in me, maybe back to the Southwest or somewhere else west across that old 100th meridian—the high desert or the central Rockies. Maybe even on up to Alaska, a place I have visited many times and wondered on each trip why I wasn't living there. I motor along, driving and thinking and thinking and driving.

Suddenly, I bring my vehicle up short because I've seen a movement out of the corner of my eye. A coyote is moving across the field, angling away from me as she makes for a break in the trees. I pull over and stop to get a better look as she moves through the corn stubble. She seems to have a bit of a limp, and there is a fringe of gray around her muzzle. There is gray around my muzzle as well, and I squint, trying to see if she is the same old girl I have been seeing from time to time in this area over the past few years. I think she is. She pauses and looks back, as coyotes are wont to do, and we stare at each other for some seconds. I'd like to believe that she recognizes me, but I doubt it. The important thing is that I recognize her, just as she turns and disappears into the under-brush.

Notes

Acknowledgments

Index

Illustration Credits

Notes

Prologue

1. The original articles by John and Frank Craighead, David Mech, Maurice Hornocker, and others can be found in *National Geographic* magazine. The first four articles listed here are the ones I refer to in the Prologue. The fifth article provides additional information on David Mech's early wolf work in the Great Lakes region of the United States. D. L. Allen and L. D. Mech, "Wolves versus Moose on Isle Royale," *National Geographic*, February 1963, 200–219; F. Craighead, Jr., and J. J. Craighead, "Knocking Out Grizzly Bears for Their Own Good," *National Geographic*, August 1960, 276–291; F. Craighead, Jr., and J. Craighead, "Trailing Yellowstone's Grizzlies by Radio," *National Geographic*, August 1966, 252–267; M. G. Hornocker and W. Wiles, "Stalking the Mountain Lion—to Save Him," *National Geographic*, November 1969, 638–655; L. D. Mech, "Where Can the Wolf Survive?" *National Geographic*, October 1977, 518–537.

2. In keeping with the older, "classic" articles in *National Geographic*, I cite Larsen's 1971 piece on polar bears. More recent information on polar bears and on Churchill, Manitoba, including the film *Polar Bear Alert*, can be found at the National Geographic Society, among other places; T. Larsen, "Polar Bear: Lonely Nomad of the North," *National Geographic*, April 1971, 574–590; National Geographic, *Polar Bear Alert* (1982), National Geographic Videos, National Geographic Society, Washington, D.C.

3. For estimates of numbers of coyotes killed for purposes of animal control, see www.aphis.usda.gov; G. E. Connolly, "Predator Control and Coyote Populations: A Review of Simulation Models," in M. Beckoff, ed., *Coyotes: Biology, Behavior, and Management* (New York: Academic Press, 1978), 327–345; and C. H. Fox and C. M. Papouchis, *Coyotes in Our Midst: Coexisting with an Adaptable and Resilient Carnivore* (Sacramento, Calif.: Animal Protection Institute, 2005). For the estimate of livestock damage see B. R. Mitchell, M. M. Jaeger, and R. H. Barrett, "Coyote Depredation Management: Current Methods and Research Needs," *Wildlife Society Bulletin* 32 (2004): 1209–1218.

1. The World's Neighborhoods

1. With the successful reintroduction of the California condor into the Grand Canyon in Arizona and sites in California, several books about it have been published in the last decade or so. I originally obtained information from a summary article: J. Cilek, "A California Condor Blessed Event," *Birdscapes*, Winter 2004, 20–21. Some books to consult include: N. F. R. Snyder and H. Snyder, *The California Condor: A Saga of Natural History and Conservation* (San Diego, Calif.: Academic Press, 2000); and J. Nielsen, *Condor: To the Brink and Back—the Life and Times of One Giant Bird* (New York: HarperCollins, 2006).

2. For more on the term "urban sprawl," see J. Black, "The Economics of Sprawl," *Urban Land* (March 1996): 52–53, as cited in T. J. Nechyba and R. P. Walsh, "Urban Sprawl," working paper, Lincoln Institute of Land Policy, Cambridge, Mass., 2004. An excellent overview of the topic of sprawl can be found in J. G. Mitchell, "Urban Sprawl," *National Geographic*, July 2001, 48–73.

3. A hectare contains 2.5 acres. For a discussion of terminology relating to urbanization, see J. M. Marzluff, R. Bowman, and R. Donnelly, "A Historical Perspective on Urban Bird Research: Trends, Terms, and Approaches," in Marzluff, Bowman, and Donnelly, eds., *Avian Ecology and Conservation in an Urbanizing World* (Boston: Kluwer Academic, 2001), 1–17.

4. Land use and urban growth in the United States is covered in R. N. Lubowski, M. Vesterby, S. Bucholtz, A. Baez, and M. J. Roberts, *Major Uses of Land in the United States, 2002*, U.S. Department of Agriculture, Economic Information Bulletin no. 14 (Washington, D.C.: U.S. Government Printing Office, 2005).

5. An Act to Establish a National Wilderness Preservation System for the Permanent Good of the Whole People, and for Other Purposes, Public Law 88–577, 88th Congress, S. 4, September 3, 1964, section 1. This act may be cited as the Wilderness Act. See http://www.wilderness.net/index.cfm. Definition from the Wilderness Act, section 1131(a).

6. Ibid., (c). Wallace Stegner wrote eloquently of both the human condition and the natural world. See letter from Stegner to David E. Pesonen of the Wildland Research Center, University of California, Berkeley, December 3, 1960, at http://wilderness.org/content/wilderness-letter. See also C. Meine, ed., *Wallace Stegner and the Continental Vision* (Washington, D.C.: Island Press, 1997).

7. O. B. Toon, "African Dust in Florida Clouds," *Nature* 424 (August 2003): 623–624; J. Whitfield, "Too Hot to Handle," *Nature* 425 (September 2003): 338–339. On the Antarctic ozone hole, see http://www.epa.gov/ozone; on the Global Monitoring Division, see http://www.esrl.noaa.gov/gmd; on the British Antarctic Survey, see http://www.antarctica.ac.uk.

8. On the increase in water temperature in the deepest areas of the North Pacific, see M. Fukasawa and others, "Bottom Water Warming in the North Pacific Ocean," *Nature* 427 (February 2004): 825–827. R. Zimmerman, *Leaving Earth: Space Stations, Rival Superpowers, and the Quest for Interplanetary Travel* (Washington, D.C.: Joseph Henry Press, 2003).

9. Gradients are a popular topic in the ecological literature, and urban-rural or urban-natural gradients have received considerable attention in the past dozen years or so. See M. J. McDonnell and S. T. A. Pickett, "Ecosystem Structure and Function along Urban-Rural Gradients: An Unexploited Opportunity for Ecology," *Ecology* 71 (1990): 1232–1237.

10. For a definition, statistics, and descriptions of land cover, see the U.S. Geological Survey Land Cover Institute, at http://landcover.usgs.gov.

11. For an alternative view on the issue of sprawl, see S. R. Staley, *The Sprawling of America: In Defense of the Dynamic City,* Policy Study no. 251 (Los Angeles: Reason Public Policy Institute, 1999), available online at http://www.reason.org/ps251.html.

12. For an overview of energy use in the United States, see U.S. Department of Energy, *Energy in the United States: 1635 to 2000,* at http://www.eia.doe.gov/emeu/aer/eh/frame.html. The statistics on home sizes in the United States were reported in *This Old House* magazine, May 2003, p. 18.

13. For more on the concept of the human footprint, see E. W. Sanderson and others, "The Human Footprint and the Last of the Wild," *BioScience* 52 (October 2002): 891–904. For an analysis of the principal anthropogenic environmental stressors and their "drivers," see also T. Dietz, E. A. Rosa, and R. York, "Driving the Human Ecological Footprint," *Frontiers in Ecology and the Environment* 5 (2007): 13–18.

14. For information on a desert city and its water, see J. Gelt and others, *Water in the Tucson Area: Seeking Sustainability,* a status report of the Water Resources Research Center (Tucson: College of Agriculture, University of Arizona, 1999), available online at http://ag.arizona.edu/azwater. P. Friederici, "Stolen River: the Colorado and Its Delta Are Losing Out," *Defenders,* Spring 1998, 11–18, 31–33. Quotation from Aldo Leopold, *A Sand County Almanac, with Other Essays on Conservation from Round River* (New York: Oxford University Press, 1966 [1949]), 148.

15. Estimates of oil consumption vary. The U.S. Department of Energy's Office of Science estimated that the United States consumed 142 billion gallons of gasoline in 2007. See http://genomicsgtl.energy.gov. Another site, http://science.howstuffworks.com/us-gas-addiction.htm, estimated that the United States uses 146 billion gallons of gasoline a year. See also the Web site of the Energy Information Administration, http://www.eia.doe.gov, for additional information. Statistics

on driving habits in the United States can be found in Bureau of Transportation Statistics, U.S. Department of Transportation, Washington, D.C., *2001 National Household Travel Survey,* http://www.bts.gov.

16. For world population figures, see Population Reference Bureau, 2009 World Population Data Sheet, and Human Population: Fundamentals of Growth and Change, both at http://www.prb.org. For information on human growth and immigration rates, see P. Salonius, "Population Growth in the United States and Canada: A Role for Scientists," *Conservation Biology* 13 (1999): 1518–1519.

17. For information on the increasing trend toward urbanized living, as well as a discussion on the size of cities, see J. E. Cohen, "Human Population: The Next Half Century," *Science,* November 2003, 1172–1175.

18. The image of the earth at night, which has been dubbed Bright Lights, Big City, can be found at Earth Observatory, the National Aeronautics and Space Administration Web site, http://earthobservatory.nasa.gov/Features/Lights.

19. See Parker's excellent book for a complete overview of the eastern coyote: Gerry Parker, *Eastern Coyote: The Story of Its Success* (Halifax, Nova Scotia: Nimbus, 1995). For a very readable and comprehensive overview on wolves, see T. K. Fuller, *Wolves of the World: Natural History and Conservation* (Stillwater, Minn.: Voyageur, 2004). Bernard DeVoto, *Across the Wide Missouri* (Boston: Houghton Mifflin, 1947), 6.

20. For information on the arrival of coyotes in Massachusetts and other parts of New England, see L. Pringle, "Notes on Coyotes in Southern New England," *Journal of Mammalogy* 41 (1960): 278.

2. The Form Setter

1. The information on estimated numbers of nesting seabirds on Round Island is included in S. Rice, "Raven Predation of Seabird Eggs at Round Island, Alaska" (M.S. thesis, University of Arizona, Tucson, 2004). For the definitive study on foxes on Round Island, see C. J. Zabel, "Reproductive Behavior of the Red Fox *(Vulpes vulpes):* A Longitudinal Study of an Island Population" (Ph.D. dissertation, University of California, Santa Cruz, 1986). For additional information on foxes on islands off the coast of Alaska, see E. P. Bailey, *Introduction of Foxes to Alaskan Islands—History, Effects on Avifauna, and Eradication,* U.S. Fish and Wildlife Service, Resource Publication 193 (Washington, D.C.: U.S. Government Printing Office, 1993).

2. Among the monumental works of Francis Fay on the walrus are F. H. Fay,

Ecology and Biology of the Pacific Walrus, Odobenus rosmarus divergens Illiger., North American Fauna, no. 74 (Washington, D.C.: U.S. Fish and Wildlife Service, U.S. Department of the Interior, 1982); and Fay, "Mammalian Species: *Odobenus rosmarus,*" *American Society of Mammalogists* 238 (1985): 1–7.

3. More information on walruses can be found at http://alaska.usgs.gov/science/biology/walrus/index.html.

4. See the excellent Web site maintained by the Watertown Historical Society (WHS), http://www.ci.watertown.ma.us/index.asp. Much of the information I used for this portion of the book comes from that site.

5. For information on the Massachuset and other Native American tribes, as well as on tribal relationships, these Web sites are a good place to start: http://www.accessgenealogy.com/native/tribes/massachuset/massachusethist.htm, http://www.indians.org, and http://www.doi.gov/bia.

6. For information on Clapp, Saltonstall, Phillips, and other aspects of regional history go to http://www.ci.watertown.ma.us/index.asp.

7. The quotation is from R. Thompson, *Divided We Stand: Watertown, Massachusetts, 1630–1680* (Amherst: University of Massachusetts Press, Amherst, 2001).

8. For information and illustrations of early development of Watertown and the area just outside of Boston, see Friends of the Watertown Free Public Library and the Historical Society of Watertown, *Watertown [MA] (Images of America)* (Charleston, S.C.: Arcadia, 2002).

9. For background on the Oakley Country Club, see *Oakley Country Club: The First 100 Years, 1898–1998: A Special Legacy* (Watertown, Mass.: Oakley Country Club, 1998).

10. For information on the Charles River, see Maud deLeigh Hodges, *Crossroads on the Charles: A History of Watertown, Massachusetts* (Canaan, N.H.: Phoenix, 1980).

11. For an interesting perspective on progress and technology, see J. Mander, *In the Absence of the Sacred* (San Francisco: Sierra Club Books, 1991).

12. For a comprehensive view of life in the United States during the 1950s, see D. Halberstam, *The Fifties* (Columbine, N.Y.: Fawcett, 1993). For a discussion of people moving in America, see J. M. Jasper, *Restless Nation: Starting Over in America* (Chicago: University of Chicago Press, 2000). Some of this information was also cited in *This Old House* magazine, June 2003, p. 24.

13. On population growth in Tucson, see http://www.censusscope.org/us/m8520/chart_popl.html.

14. On coyote movements and other aspects of natural history in North America, see M. Bekoff and E. M. Gese, "Coyote, *Canis latrans,*" in G. A. Feldhamer, B. C. Thompson, and J. A. Chapman, eds., *Wild Mammals of North Amer-*

ica: Biology, Management, and Conservation, 2nd ed. (Baltimore: Johns Hopkins University Press, 2003), 467–481, esp. table 22.4 on 472. For specific information on home range and movement, as well as other aspects of natural history specific to coyotes in the Northeast, see M. E. Gompper, *The Ecology of Northeast Coyotes: Current Knowledge and Priorities for Future Research,* working paper no. 17 (The Bronx, N.Y.: Wildlife Conservation Society, 2002). The quotation is from Bekoff and Gese, "Coyote, *Canis latrans,*" 470.

15. Bekoff and Gese, "Coyote, *Canis latrans.*"

16. G. Parker, *Eastern Coyote: The Story of Its Success* (Halifax, Nova Scotia: Nimbus, 1995).

17. M. Grinder and P. R. Krausman, "Home Range, Habitat Use, and Nocturnal Activity of Coyotes in an Urban Environment," *Journal of Wildlife Management* 65 (2001): 887–898; J. G. Way, I. M. Ortega, and P. J. Auger, "Eastern Coyote Home Range, Territoriality, and Sociality on Urbanized Cape Cod," *Northeast Wildlife* 57 (2002): 1–18. According to Parker, *Eastern Coyote,* and other authorities, coyotes are present in every state except Hawaii. For a perspective on coyote management and summary of his urban coyote research, see J. G. Way, *Suburban Howls: Tracking the Eastern Coyote in Urban Massachusetts* (Indianapolis: Dog Ear, 2007).

3. Gradient in Time

1. K. Ross, *Okavango: Jewel of the Kalahari* (New York: Macmillan, 1987). J. Kingdon, *The Kingdon Field Guide to African Mammals* (London: A & C Black, 2003), lists 111 species of ungulates out of 1,150 total mammal species. F. Reid, *The Field Guide to Mammals of North America* (Boston: Houghton Mifflin, 2006), lists 15 species of ungulates out of about 335 land mammal species, so the ratio is actually more like seven ungulates in Africa to every one in North America. L. Ramberg and others, "Species Diversity of the Okavango Delta, Botswana," *Aquatic Sciences* 68, no. 3 (October 2006): 310–337.

2. For information on biodiversity, see E. O. Wilson, ed., *Biodiversity* (Washington, D.C.: National Academy, 1988); Wilson, *The Diversity of Life* (New York: Norton, 1999); and other writings by Wilson.

3. For a discussion of history and nature, see W. Cronan, "Modes of Prophecy and Production: Placing Nature in History," *Journal of American History* 76 (1990): 1122–1131; and Cronan, "A Place for Stories: Nature, History, and Narrative," *Journal of American History* 78 (1992): 1347–1376.

4. For the history of the Hudson Bay Company and the North American fur

trade, as well as the natural history of the beaver, see G. Bryce, *The Remarkable History of the Hudson Bay Company*, reprint (New York: Burt Franklin, 1968 [1904]).

5. For information on the passenger pigeon, see David E. Blockstein, "Passenger Pigeon (*Ectopistes migratorius*)," in A. Poole, ed., *The Birds of North America* (Ithaca, N.Y.: Cornell Lab of Ornithology, 2002), available online at http://bna.birds.cornell.edu/bna/species/611; A. W. Eckert, *The Silent Sky: The Incredible Extinction of the Passenger Pigeon* (Lincoln, Neb.: iUniverse.com, 2000); and A. W. Schroger, *The Passenger Pigeon: Its History and Extinction* (Caldwell, N.J.: Blackburn, 2004).

6. For a general overview of state wildlife laws, see R. S. Musgrave and M. A. Stein, *State Wildlife Laws Handbook* (Rockville, Md.: Government Institutes Inc., 1993), 6–13, online at http://www.animallaw.info/articles/arusHistoryStateWM.htm. Aldo Leopold, *Game Management* (New York: Charles Scribner's Sons, 1933).

7. On the human and natural history of North America, as well as changes in the landscape, see W. Cronan, *Changes in the Land: Indians, Colonists, and the Ecology of New England* (New York: Hill and Wang, 1983); D. Worster, *Under Western Skies: Nature and History in the American West* (New York: Oxford University Press, 1994); M. T. Watts, *Reading the Landscape of America* (Rochester, N.Y.: Nature Study Guild, 1999); and D. R. Foster and others, "Insights from Historical Geography to Ecology and Conservation: Lessons from the New England Landscape," *Journal of Biogeography* 29, nos. 10/11 (October/November 2002), special issue.

8. On the history of urban ecology, see L. W. Adams, "Urban Wildlife Ecology and Conservation: A Brief History of the Discipline," *Urban Ecosystems* 8 (2005): 139–156; and C. H. Nilon, A. R. Berkowitz, and K. S. Hollweg, "Understanding Urban Ecosystems: A New Frontier for Science and Education," *Urban Ecosystems* 3 (1999): 3–4.

9. Chimney swifts in colonial chimneys are mentioned in J. Josselyn, *New England's Rarities Discovered*, reprint (Boston: W. Veaze, 1860 [1672]).

10. Early studies on urban wildlife include W. L. McAtee, *How to Attract Birds in Northeastern United States* (Washington, D.C.: U.S. Department of Agriculture, 1914); Leopold, *Game Management*; D. W. Lay, "Ecology of the Opossum," *Journal of Mammalogy* 23 (1942): 147–158; and L. G. Brown and L. E. Yeager. "Fox Squirrels and Gray Squirrels in Illinois," *Bulletin of the Illinois Natural History Survey* 23 (1945): 449–536. See S. DeStefano and R. M. DeGraaf, "Exploring the Ecology of Suburban Wildlife," *Frontiers in Ecology and the Environment* 1 (2003): 95–101, for a partial historical review.

11. W. Erz, "Ecological Principles in the Urbanization of Birds," *Ostrich*, suppl. 6 (1966): 357–363.

12. Bureau of Sport Fisheries and Wildlife, U.S. Department of the Interior, *Man and Nature in the City* (Washington, D.C.: U.S. Government Printing Office, 1968); J. H. Noyes and D. R. Progulske, eds., *Wildlife in an Urbanizing Environment* (Amherst: Cooperative Extension Service, University of Massachusetts, 1974); D. Euler, F. Gilbert, and G. McKeating, eds., *Wildlife in Urban Canada* (Guelph, Ontario: Office of Continuing Education, University of Guelph, and Ontario Ministry of Natural Resources, 1975); D. L. Leedy, ed., *An Annotated Bibliography on Planning and Management for Urban-Suburban Wildlife* (Washington, D.C.: 1979).

13. Two colleagues, both of whom were engaged in the field and have conducted research and written on the subject extensively, support the observation that interest in urban wildlife waned during the 1980s. Personal communications with Dr. Richard M. DeGraaf and Dr. Lowell W. Adams.

14. For an in-depth discussion of the spotted owl and old-growth logging issues, see S. L. Yaffee, *The Wisdom of the Spotted Owl: Policy Lessons for a New Century* (Washington, D.C.: Island Press, 1994).

15. For an overview, see D. J. Decker, T. L. Brown, and W. F. Siemer, eds., *Human Dimensions of Wildlife Management in North America* (Bethesda, Md.: Wildlife Society, 2001). See also MassWildlife's Web site at http://www.mass.gov/dfwele /dfw/dfw_toc.htm; and the Web sites of other state wildlife agencies for a trove of information about wildlife, including urban and suburban wildlife, living with wildlife, problem wildlife, and so on.

16. For summaries and an extensive list of literature on diet, as well as an excellent review of coyote predation on deer, see G. Parker, *Eastern Coyote: The Story of Its Success* (Halifax, Nova Scotia: Nimbus, 1995).

17. For information on the diet of urban coyotes, see S. Gehrt, *Urban Coyote Ecology and Management: The Cook County, Illinois, Coyote Project,* bulletin 929 (n.d.), Ohio State University Extension, Columbus.

18. Statistics on human fatalities based on information from the National Safety Council (2002), www.nsc.org, and from R. D. Deblinger and S. DeStefano, "Predator Attacks," *Massachusetts Wildlife* 51 (2006): 4–9.

4. Suburban Wildlife Encounters

1. The image of the only person walking at the top of the world was one I first saw in Thomas Hardy's beautifully written *Far from the Madding Crowd* (London: Smith, Elder, 1874).

2. Among the articles related to the cougar attack on a woman near John-sondale, California, see "Cougar Mauls Woman on Hike," *Los Angeles Times,* June 28, 2004; "Attack by a Mountain Lion Costs Santa Monica Hiker Her Right Eye," *San Diego Union-Tribune,* June 28, 2004; and "Mountain Lion That Attacked Hiker Was Undernourished," *San Diego Union-Tribune,* June 28, 2004. For an overview of coyote attacks on people, see R. M. Timm, R. O. Baker, J. R. Bennett, and C. C. Coolahan, "Coyote Attacks: An Increasing Suburban Problem," *Transactions of the North American Wildlife and Natural Resources Conference* 69 (2004): 67–88.

3. For a perspective on the rarity of predator attacks on people, see R. D. Deblinger and S. DeStefano, "Predator Attacks," *Massachusetts Wildlife* 56, no. 2 (2006): 4–9.

4. For a discussion of the issues that arise when increasing numbers of people move into rural areas or wildlife habitat, see R. E. Heimlich and W. D. Anderson, *Development at the Urban Fringe and Beyond: Impacts on Agriculture and Rural Land* (Washington, D.C.: U.S. Department of Agriculture, 2001); and B. L. Lawrence, "The Context and Causes of Sprawl," in E. A. Johnson and M. W. Klemens, eds., *Nature in Fragments: The Legacy of Sprawl* (New York: Columbia University Press, 2005), 3–17.

5. For a discussion of species that can do well in urbanizing environments, see S. DeStefano and E. A. Johnson, "Species That Benefit from Sprawl," in Johnson and Klemens, *Nature in Fragments,* 206–235.

6. For a detailed discussion of fear and learning in wild animals, see J. Berger, *The Better to Eat You With: Fear in the Animal World* (Chicago: University of Chicago Press, 2008).

7. For a thorough treatment of the issues surrounding conflicts between human beings and wildlife, and potential solutions for dealing with those problems, see M. Conover, *Resolving Human-Wildlife Conflicts: The Science of Wildlife Damage Management* (Washington, D.C.: Lewis, 2002).

8. See S. DeStefano and R. D. Deblinger, "Wildlife as Valuable Natural Resources versus Intolerable Pests: A Suburban Wildlife Management Model," *Urban Ecosystems* 8 (2005): 179–190.

9. For an introduction to "cultural carrying capacity" and similar concepts, see L. H. Carpenter, D. J. Decker, and J. F. Lipscomb, "Stakeholder Acceptance Capacity in Wildlife Management," *Human Dimensions of Wildlife* 5 (2000): 5–19; and H. C. Zinn, M. J. Manfredo, and J. J. Vaske, "Social Psychological Bases for Stakeholder Acceptance Capacity," *Human Dimensions of Wildlife* 5 (2000): 20–33. For a thorough review of the concept of "overabundant" species and their management as applied to deer, see W. J. McShea, H. B. Underwood, and J. H. Rappole, eds., *The*

Science of Overabundance: Deer Ecology and Population Management (Washington, D.C.: Smithsonian Institution Press, 1997).

10. A very important book for anyone interested in hunting, from either a pro- or an antihunting perspective, is R. Nelson, *Heart and Blood: Living with Deer in America* (New York: Knopf, 1997).

11. For an interesting and important case history on wildlife management through public referendum, see R. D. Deblinger, W. A. Woytek, and R. R. Zwick, "Demographics of Voting on the 1996 Massachusetts Ballot Referendum," *Human Dimensions of Wildlife* 4 (1999): 40–55.

12. On the question of whether those who hunt and fish can work together with birdwatchers and hikers: it should be recognized that these activities are not mutually exclusive and that a great many individuals engage in all these pastimes.

13. On the changing role of the mountain lion, see DeStefano and Deblinger, "Wildlife as Valuable Natural Resources."

14. For some of the first ecological studies of the North American mountain lion, see M. G. Hornocker, "An Analysis of Mountain Lion Predation upon Mule Deer and Elk in the Idaho Primitive Area," *Wildlife Monograph* 21 (1970); J. C. Seidensticker, M. G. Hornocker, W. V. Wiles, and J. P. Messick, "Mountain Lion Social Organization in the Idaho Primitive Area," *Wildlife Monograph* 35 (1973); and M. G. Hornocker, "Stalking the Mountain Lion—to Save Him," *National Geographic,* November 1969, 638–655.

15. For a list of mountain lion attacks on humans, see "Mountain Lion Attacks on People in the U.S. and Canada," at http://tchester.org/sgm/lists/lion_attacks.html.

16. For mention of works that discuss communication among coyotes, including legends about it, see J. F. Dobie, *The Voice of the Coyote* (Boston: Little, Brown, 1949); and H. Ryden, *God's Dog: A Celebration of the North American Coyote* (Bloomington, Ind.: iUniverse, 2005).

5. Mixed Messages

1. U.S. Food and Drug Administration, Center for Food Safety and Applied Nutrition, "The Food Defect Action Levels: Levels of Natural or Unavoidable Defects in Foods that Present No Health Hazards for Humans" (Rockville, Md.: USFDA Center for Food Safety and Applied Nutrition, 1998), available online at http://vm.cfsan.fda.gov/~dms/dalbook.html#CHPT1. See also M. Roach, "Bug Heads, Rat Hairs—Bon Appétit," 2000, at http://archive.salon.com/health/col/

roac/2000/01/14/filth_lab/print.html, for a humorous and enlightening look at the topic.

2. *Eukaryotes in Extreme Environments,* comp. Dave Roberts, Department of Zoology, Natural History Museum, London SW7 5BD, U.K., 5 February 1998, at http://www.nhm.ac.uk/zoology/extreme.html#Mar70. See also M. T. Madigan and B. L. Marrs, "Extremophiles," *Scientific American,* April 1997, 82–87; and K. Horikoshi and W. D. Grant, eds., *Extremophiles—Microbial Life in Extreme Environments* (New York: Plenum, 1998).

3. J. Kieran, *A Natural History of New York City* (Boston: Houghton Mifflin, 1959), including the quote which begins, "Let the population of the area increase."

4. A discussion of the various ways in which species may respond to urbanization can be found in S. DeStefano and R. M. DeGraaf, "Exploring the Ecology of Suburban Wildlife," *Frontiers in Ecology and the Environment* 1 (2003): 95–101.

5. See R. F. Johnston, "Synanthropic Birds of North America," in J. M. Marzluff, R. Bowman, and R. Donnelly, eds., *Avian Ecology and Conservation in an Urbanizing World* (Boston: Kluwer Academic, 2001), 49–67, for a definition and discussion of synanthropy.

6. An enjoyable book about one of the most synanthropic species and highly successful residents of New York City is R. Sullivan, *Rats: Observations on the History and Habitat of the City's Most Unwanted Inhabitants* (New York: Bloomsbury, 2004).

7. For research on urbanization and carnivores, see S. P. D. Riley and others, "Effects of Urbanization and Habitat Fragmentation on Bobcats and Coyotes in Southern California," *Conservation Biology* 17 (2003): 566–576; R. Woodroffe, "Predators and People: Using Human Densities to Interpret Declines of Large Ungulates," *Animal Conservation* 3 (2006): 165–173; and S. D. Gehrt, S. P. D. Riley, and B. L. Cypher, *Urban Carnivores: Ecology, Conflict, and Conservation* (Baltimore: Johns Hopkins University Press, 2010).

8. "The greatest wonder of this planet" is quoted from E. O. Wilson, ed., *Biodiversity* (Washington, D.C.: National Academy Press, 1988), v.

9. For one study of mortality on roads, see J. P. Gibbs and W. G. Shriver, "Estimating the Effects of Road Mortality on Turtle Populations," *Conservation Biology* 16 (2002): 1647–1652.

10. Many researchers suggest that it takes groups or packs of two or more coyotes to hunt deer successfully, and that local snow conditions (that is, deep snow) aid coyotes in their predation on deer. Patterson and Messier (2000) reported, however, that during their study of coyotes and white-tailed deer in Nova Scotia single coyotes killed more than sixteen deer (23 percent of all kills for which coy-

ote group size was known). B. R. Patterson and F. Messier, "Factors Influencing Killing Rates of White-tailed Deer by Coyotes in Eastern Canada," *Journal of Wildlife Management* 64 (2000): 721–732.

6. The Suburban Jungle

1. For a complete account on the life history and ecology of roadrunners, including their calls, see J. M. Hughes, "Greater Roadrunner (*Geococcyx californianus*)," in A. Poole, ed., *The Birds of North America* (Ithaca, N.Y.: Cornell Lab of Ornithology, 1996). See also C. M. Webster and S. DeStefano, "Using Public Surveys to Determine the Distribution of Greater Roadrunners in Urban and Suburban Tucson, Arizona," in W. W. Shaw, L. K. Harris, and L. VanDruff, eds., *Urban Wildlife Conservation*, Proceedings of the 4th International Symposium, Tucson, Ariz., pp. 69–77; and S. DeStefano and C. M. Webster, "Distribution and Habitat of Greater Roadrunners in Urban and Suburban Tucson, Arizona," *Studies in Avian Biology* (in press) for information on roadrunners in an urban environment.

2. Regarding bats in your house, it is never a good idea to let any of these or other animals really colonize your home. Damage of some sort is a likely outcome, and disease is always a potential concern. I don't worry too much about a bat or two up under the fascia boards, but the best approach is to prevent access in the first place by repairing all holes and blocking other entry points. Check the Web for innovative techniques that will allow animals one-way travel out but will prevent them from coming back in, and for other tips on keeping animals out of your home.

3. The term "habitat" has been used to describe the place where an animal lives. Thus, the habitat of the red eft is the moist forest floor. The green heron lives in and around emergent wetlands. The javelina's haunt is the desert. We often equate habitat with some kind of vegetation, and so we speak of forest habitat or grassland habitat. The *concept* of habitat, however, is a little bit different. In the scientific literature you will see "habitat" defined as the sum total of all the physical features of the environment that a species needs for its entire life. This includes but is not limited to vegetation. So, for example, a migratory warbler's habitat includes nesting areas in the northern United States and Canada, wintering areas in Latin America, and all the migratory stopover areas in between for both spring and fall migration. Take away any one of those components and the species would be in trouble. Furthermore, habitat is species-specific. To a practicing biologist, then, it makes sense to talk about wood duck habitat or bullfrog habitat or water strider habitat, but if you say "wetland habitat," the biologist might ask, "For

which species?" because not all species that use wetlands have the same habitat. Confusing, I know. Someone once said that terminology is to biology what equations are to engineering, which doesn't really help. To make matters worse, even biologists use the word "habitat" in both ways: the species-specific habitat-as-concept way, and the general everyday usage of "habitat" as a place where an animal lives. I rely on this dual use for the term as regards urban or suburban habitat. Just keep in mind the many species that live in urban and suburban environments, each species with its own specific habitat in which it can exist. See L. S. Hall, P. R. Krausman, and M. L. Morrison, "The Habitat Concept and a Plea for Standard Terminology," *Wildlife Society Bulletin* 25 (1997): 173–182; D. L. Garshelis, "Delusions in Habitat Evaluation: Measuring Use, Selection, and Importance," in L. Boitani and T. K. Fuller, eds., *Research Techniques in Animal Ecology* (New York: Columbia University Press, 2000), 111–164; and M. L. Morrison, B. G. Marcot, and R. W. Mannan, *Wildlife-Habitat Relationships,* 3rd ed. (Washington, D.C.: Island Press, 2006).

4. *This Old House* is a long-running, award-winning home improvement television show on the Public Broadcasting System (PBS).

5. Comprehensive treatments of urban habitat can be found in L. W. Adams, *Urban Wildlife Habitats: A Landscape Perspective* (Minneapolis: University of Minnesota Press, 1994), and C. E. Adams, K. J. Lindsey, and S. J. Ash, *Urban Wildlife Management* (Boca Raton, Fla.: Taylor and Francis, 2006).

6. R. H. MacArthur and E. O. Wilson, *The Theory of Island Biogeography,* Monographs in Population Biology, no. 1 (Princeton, N.J.: Princeton University Press, 1967).

7. For information on urban sprawl and the spread of non-native species, see M. A. Withers and others, "Changing Patterns in the Number of Species in North American Floras," in T. D. Sisk, ed., *Perspectives on the Land Use History of North America: A Context for Understanding Our Changing Environment* (Washington, D.C.: U.S. Geological Survey, 1998).

8. For a discussion of invasive species and recombinant ecology and communities, see M. E. Soulé, "The Onslaught of Alien Species, and Other Challenges in the Coming Decades," *Conservation Biology* 4 (1990): 233–239. See also J. E. Byers, "Impact of Non-indigenous Species on Natives Enhanced by Anthropogenic Alteration of Selection Regimes," *Oikos* 97 (2002): 449–458, and S. DeStefano and E. A. Johnson, "Species that Benefit from Sprawl," in E. A. Johnson and M. E. Klemens, eds., *Nature in Fragments: The Legacy of Sprawl* (New York: Columbia University Press, 2005), 206–235.

9. S. H. Faeth, P. S. Warren, E. Shochat, and W. A. Marussich, "Trophic Dynamics in Urban Communities," *BioScience* 55 (2005): 399–407.

10. For excellent examples of research on urban raptors, see C. W. Boal and R. W. Mannan, "Nest-Site Selection by Cooper's Hawks in an Urban Environment," *Journal of Wildlife Management* 62 (1998): 864–871; and C. W. Boal and R. W. Mannan, "Comparative Breeding Ecology of Cooper's Hawks in Urban and Exurban Areas of Southeastern Arizona," *Journal of Wildlife Management* 63 (1999): 77–84.

11. J. H. Falk, "Energetics of a Suburban Lawn Ecosystem," *Ecology* 57 (1976): 141–150.

12. Use of lawns by Canada geese is discussed in M. R. Conover, "Herbivory by Canada Geese: Diet Selection and Effect on Lawns," *Ecological Applications* 1 (1991): 231–236.

13. For information on the amount of area covered by grass, see R. Lindsey, *Looking for Lawns* (Greenbelt, Md.: NASA Earth Observatory, 2005), online at http://earthobservatory.nasa.gov/Study/Lawn/printall.php; and C. Milesi and others, "Mapping and Modeling the Biogeochemical Cycling of Turf Grasses in the United States," *Environmental Management* 36 (2005): 426–438.

14. A good book on lawns is T. Steinberg, *American Green: The Obsessive Quest for the Perfect Lawn* (New York: Norton, 2006).

15. See "Lawns Offer Good News for the Environment," at www.landcare network.org, or search the Internet for the title.

16. 1990 Farm Bill—Food, Agriculture, Conservation, and Trade Act, National Agricultural Law Center, www.nationalaglawcenter.org.

17. April is National Lawn Care Month, as promoted by the Professional Landcare Network (PLANET), LandcareNetwork.org. When the Associated Landscape Contractors of America (ALCA) and the Professional Lawn Care Association of America (PLCAA) combined in 2005, PLANET was formed.

18. For information on coyote mortality, see G. Parker, *Eastern Coyote: The Story of Its Success* (Halifax, Nova Scotia: Nimbus, 1995); M. Grinder and P. R. Krausman, "Morbidity-Mortality Factors and Survival of an Urban Coyote Population in Arizona," *Journal of Wildlife Diseases* 37 (2001): 312–317; M. E. Gompper, *The Ecology of Northeast Coyotes,* working paper no. 17 (The Bronx, N.Y.: Wildlife Conservation Society, 2002); and S. D. Gehrt, *Urban Coyote Ecology and Management: The Cook County, Illinois, Coyote Project,* Bulletin 929 (Columbus: Ohio State University, n.d.).

7. A Trilogy of Tolerable Nuisances, Part 1: Traffic

1. S. DeStefano, "Observations of Kit Foxes in Southeastern Oregon," *Northwestern Naturalist* 73 (1992): 54–56.

2. L. Miller, "Cars Outnumber Household Drivers," *Recorder,* Greenfield, Mass., 23–30 August 2003, p. 16.

3. Figures on per capita car ownership throughout the world vary; these statistics were taken from the Energy Information Administration, International Energy Outlook 2001, "World Per Capita Vehicle Ownership by Region, 1990–2020," as reported by Iowa Public Television, www.iptv.org/exploremore/energy/features/fworld.cfm.

4. J. G. Mitchell, "Urban Sprawl," *National Geographic,* July 2001, 48–73.

5. R. T. T. Forman and others, *Road Ecology, Science and Solutions* (Washington, D.C.: Island, 2003).

6. The familiar joke runs like this: When an outsider who has lost his way asks an old farmer for directions, the local thinks for a bit, has trouble giving directions, and finally tells the traveler, "You can't get there from here."

7. A discussion of dirt roads versus paved roads in Maine was presented on the television program "Main Streets, Back Roads: Maine Wilderness" on *Chronicle,* WCVB-TV, Channel 5, Boston, on Monday, 9 August 2004.

8. According to http://www.ourforests.org/fact/road_construction.pdf, we have 382,000 miles of roads in the National Forest systems, including more than 50,000 miles of unclassified roads.

9. The U.S. Department of Transportation, Federal Highway Administration, reports that there are about 160,000 miles in the National Highway System, which includes only 4 percent of the nation's roads but carries more than 40 percent of all highway traffic, 75 percent of heavy truck traffic, and 90 percent of tourist traffic. See http://www.tfhrc.gov/pubrds/spring96/p96sp2.htm and http://www.fhwa.dot.gov/planning/nhs.

10. R. T. T. Forman, "Estimate of the Area Affected Ecologically by the Road System of the United States," *Conservation Biology* 14 (2000): 31–35.

11. R. T. T. Forman and R. D. Deblinger, "The Ecological Road-Effect Zone of a Massachusetts (U.S.A.) Suburban Highway," *Conservation Biology* 14 (2000): 36–46.

12. S. C. Trombulak and C. A. Frissell, "Review of Ecological Effects of Roads on Terrestrial and Aquatic Communities," *Conservation Biology* 14 (2000): 18–30.

13. U.S. Environmental Protection Agency, Heat Island Effect, http://www.epa.gov/heatisland/.

14. A. M. Farmer, "The Effects of Dust on Vegetation—A Review," *Environmental Pollution* 79 (1993): 63–75. See also Trombulak and Frissell, "Review of Ecological Effects of Roads." Effects of roads on vegetation are discussed by N. A. Auerbach, M. D. Walker, and D. A. Walker, "Effects of Roadside Disturbance on Substrate and Vegetation Properties in Arctic Tundra," *Ecological Applications* 7 (1997): 218–235.

15. You can find information on moose-vehicle collisions at the Maine Department of Transportation's Web site, http://www.maine.gov/mdot/safetyoffice/maine-crash-data.php, and the Alaska Department of Transportation's Web site, http://www.dot.state.ak.us (search on moose).

16. D. A. Steen and J. P. Gibbs, "Effects of Roads on the Structure of Freshwater Turtle Populations," *Conservation Biology* 18 (2004): 1143–1148.

17. See Trombulak and Frissell, "Review of Ecological Effects of Roads," for information on roads and changes in animal behavior.

18. A. P. Clevenger and N. Waltho, "Factors Influencing the Effectiveness of Wildlife Underpasses in Banff National Park, Alberta, Canada," *Conservation Biology* 14 (2000): 47–56.

19. Some of the background on coyote pair formation comes from G. Parker, *Eastern Coyote: The Story of Its Success* (Halifax, Nova Scotia: Nimbus, 1995).

8. A Trilogy of Tolerable Nuisances, Parts 2 and 3: Light and Noise

1. R. Kram and T. J. Dawson, "Energetics and Biomechanics of Locomotion by Red Kangaroos (*Macropus rufus*)," *Comparative Biochemistry and Physiology, Part B: Biochemistry and Molecular Biology* 120 (May 1998): 41–49.

2. See http://www.darksky.org for much more information on light pollution and related topics.

3. M. Muro, "Development Blocked Near Tucson Telescopes," *Science* 283 (January 1999): 469.

4. *The Right Stuff* (1983) was produced by Irwin Winkler and Robert Chartoff and directed by Philip Kaufman, the Ladd Company, through Warner Brothers Movies.

5. Regarding society's views on ecological goods and services, the idea that these benefits are free and can be taken for granted may be changing in light of current realizations about global climate change, rising energy costs, and the struggle for sustainability.

6. Quoted in Muro, "Development Blocked Near Tucson Telescopes."

7. For background on awareness of light pollution see R. J. Bazell, "Star Bright, Street Light, Which Will They See Tonight?" *Science* 171 (February 1971): 461.

8. T. Longcore and C. Rich, "Ecological Light Pollution," *Frontiers in Ecology and the Environment* 2 (2004): 191–198; and C. Rich and T. Longcore, eds., *Ecological Consequences of Artificial Night Lighting* (Washington, D.C.: Island Press, 2005).

9. For discussion of light and behavior and biological cycles, see S. Guynup, "Light Pollution Taking Toll on Wildlife, Eco-groups Say," *National Geographic Today,* April 17, 2003, at http://news.nationalgeographic.com/news/2003/04/0417 _030417_tvlightpollution.html.

10. J. Rydell, "Exploitation of Insects around Streetlamps by Bats in Sweden," *Functional Ecology* 6 (1992): 744–750.

11. For these figures (95 percent in fact exist with some form of light pollution), go to http://inhabitat.com/blog/2006/08/19/light-pollution-the-continuing-spread.

12. Quoted at http://www.hhmi.org/news/rosbash.html.

13. Barred owls are best known for their call of "Who cooks for you?" You can often hear their single calls, though, during the night—longer, somewhat drawn-out, and piercing.

14. Quotations on noise pollution in J. L. Hildebrand, "Noise Pollution: An Introduction to the Problem and an Outline for Future Legal Research," *Columbia Law Review* 70, no. 4 (1970): 652–692; and D. F. Anthrop, "The Noise Crisis," *University of Toronto Law Journal* 20, no. 1 (1970): 1–17.

15. H. Slabbekoorn and M. Peet, "Birds Sing at a Higher Pitch in Urban Noise," *Nature* 424 (July 2003): 267.

16. F. E. Rheindt, "The Impact of Roads on Birds: Does Song Frequency Play a Role in Determining Susceptibility to Noise Pollution?" *Journal of Ornithology* 144 (2003): 295–306.

17. See P. R. Krausman and others, *Effects of Military Operations on Behavior and Hearing of Endangered Sonoran Pronghorn,* Wildlife Monographs no. 157, 2004, for information on the relationship of noise, including military operations, and wildlife.

18. On hearing tests for polar bears by Peter Bowes, BBC News, San Diego, see http://news.bbc.co.uk/cbbcnews/hi/newsid_7640000/newsid_7644300/7644397 .stm, 30 September 2008.

19. P. S. Warren and others, "Urban Bioacoustics: It's Not Just Noise," *Animal Behaviour* 71 (2006): 491–502.

20. Some of the coyote behavior during mating is described in G. Parker, *Eastern Coyote: The Story of Its Success* (Halifax, Nova Scotia: Nimbus, 1995).

9. Home Ownership and Other Near-Death Experiences

1. See N. Marcy, G. Rutherford, and A. Mills, *Hazard Screening Report: Power Tools and Workshop Equipment* (Washington, D.C.: Consumer Product Safety

Commission, 2003), www.cpsc.gov/library/foia/foia04/os/2003h054.pdf; and on falls, the National Safety Council Web site, www.nsc.org/research/odds.aspx.

2. T. Conuel, *Quabbin, the Accidental Wilderness,* rev. ed. (Amherst: University of Massachusetts Press, 1990).

3. A. Leopold, *A Sand County Almanac* (New York: Oxford University Press, 1966 [1949]), 183.

4. On denning behavior, see G. Parker, *Eastern Coyote: The Story of Its Success* (Halifax, Nova Scotia: Nimbus, 1995).

10. A Short Story about a Small Moose

1. Some of the insights on coyote pup and denning behavior were drawn from G. Parker, *Eastern Coyote: The Story of Its Success* (Halifax, Nova Scotia: Nimbus, 1995).

11. Coyote Spirits

1. D. O. Hyde, *Don Coyote* (Boulder, Colo.: Johnson Books, 1986). Hyde came upon the main character, a local coyote that he named Don Coyote, and believed he had been killed. Don Coyote recovered from his wounds, however, and lives throughout the rest of Hyde's book, which is an excellent account of coyotes, nature, and the ranching life.

2. S. P. Young and H. H. T. Jackson, *The Clever Coyote* (Lincoln: University of Nebraska Press, 1951); H. Ryden, *God's Dog: A Celebration of the North American Coyote* (Bloomington, Ind.: iUniverse, 2005) discuss the many names that both Native Americans and European settlers have given to the coyote.

3. For insights into occasional interesting associations between coyotes and badgers, see S. Aughey, "Curious Companionship of the Coyote and the Badger," *American Naturalist* 18 (1884): 644–645; V. H. Cahalane, "Badger-Coyote 'Partnerships,'" *Journal of Mammalogy* 31 (1950): 354–355; and S. C. Minta, K. A. Minta, and D. F. Lott, "Hunting Associations between Badgers (*Taxidea taxus*) and Coyotes (*Canis latrans*)," *Journal of Mammalogy* 73 (1992): 814–820; but see also A. P. Rathbun, M. C. Wells, and M. Bekoff, "Cooperative Predation by Coyotes on Badgers," *Journal of Mammalogy* 61 (1980): 375–376. For an overview of coyote hybridization among canid species, see T. K. Fuller, *Wolves of the World: Natural History and Conservation* (Stillwater, Minn.: Voyageur, 2004).

4. See R. L. Phillips and G. L. Nunley, "Historical Perspective on Coyote Con-

trol Methods in Texas," in D. Rollins and others, eds., *Coyotes in the Southwest: A Compendium of Our Knowledge*, 13–14 December 1995 in San Angelo, Texas (http://texnat.tamu.edu/symposia/coyote/). Poisons that have been used on coyotes include cyanide, sodium fluoroacetate, and strychnine. Cyanide is any chemical compound that contains the cyano group, which consists of a carbon atom triple-bonded to a nitrogen atom. Of the many kinds of cyanide compounds, some are gases, others are solids or liquids. Those which can release the cyanide ion CN^- are highly toxic. The M44 cyanide device (also called a cyanide gun or cyanide trap) lures predators with an appealing smell, often from a small piece of bait, then makes use of a spring to propel a dose of sodium cyanide into the predator's mouth. The sodium cyanide combines with water in the mouth to produce poisonous cyanide gas. The M44 was invented in the 1960s to replace a different device, colloquially known as a coyote getter, which made use of powdered cyanide ejected by a primer. Sodium fluoroacetate (also known as sodium monofluoroacetate, or compound 1080) is a potent but nonpersistent metabolic poison that occurs naturally as an antiherbivore metabolite in various plants. It works by interfering with the citric acid cycle, and it is used primarily to control mammalian pests, including invasive species. Compound 1080 was placed in baited sheep collars; coyotes punctured the collar and ingested fatal doses when they seized sheep by the neck. Strychnine is a very toxic, colorless crystalline alkaloid used as a pesticide, particularly for killing small vertebrates such as birds and rodents. Sodium monofluoroacetate or strychnine is mixed with meat baits and placed in locations frequented by coyotes. Sometimes these poisoned baits were used on rodents, which were then ingested by coyotes. The use of many of these compounds and devices is now restricted or illegal. The .222 was and still is a popular caliber for "varmint" hunting. Hunters and predator control agents have also used larger calibers, such as .308 and .306 ("30-aught-6") for shooting coyotes. Other calibers are used as well.

12. A Suburban Land Ethic

1. The first sentence in the Foreword to Aldo Leopold's *Sand County Almanac* is "There are some who can live without wild things, and some who cannot." Aldo Leopold, *A Sand County Almanac, and Sketches Here and There* (New York: Oxford University Press, 1968 [1949]).

2. Ibid., 203–204.

3. Ibid., 204.

4. Ibid., viii.

5. Ibid., viii–ix.

6. Ibid., 203–204.

7. The concept of a paradigm shift was first discussed by T. S. Kuhn, *The Structure of Scientific Revolutions* (Chicago: University of Chicago Press, 1962).

8. Information on conservation subdivisions can be found in R. G. Arendt, *Conservation Design for Subdivisions* (Washington, D.C.: Island Press, 1996); and Metropolitan Area Planning Council, "The Conservation Subdivision Design Project: Booklet for Developing a Local Bylaw" (Boston: Executive Office of Environmental Affairs, 2000), at www.mapc.org.

Acknowledgments

Many people were more than helpful and beyond patient during the time it took me to compile, write, and revise this work. Chief among them was Ann Downer-Hazell, former editor for the Life Sciences and Health with Harvard University Press. During our time together Ann was incredibly insightful, encouraging, and above all, patient. I can't thank her enough and I can't help thinking that if more writers had editors like Ann, there would be more productive and happy writers. After Ann left, Susan Abel reviewed the entire manuscript and made many needed and worthwhile changes. There is little doubt that *Coyote* reads better because of her talent and hard work. Susan's efforts went beyond the correcting of sentence structure and pronoun-antecedent agreement (which was certainly needed!) to the core of the writing and the spirit of the message that I was striving for in the book; for that I am especially grateful. Michael Fisher, Anne Zarrella, and Christine Thorsteinsson, also of Harvard University Press, assisted in seeing the manuscript through to completion; it was a real pleasure to work with all of them as well.

I appreciate the efforts of Stephanie E. Koontz of the Ethics Office and Dr. Mike Tome of the Cooperative Research Unit Program, U.S. Department of the Interior, U.S. Geological Survey, for their guidance, understanding, and support at the beginning of this undertaking, all of which helped me navigate the paperwork and ethical considerations involved in the writing of the book.

Several people read the manuscript and were not only constructive with their comments but also very kind in their critiques. These readers included Susan Copithorne, Rob Deblinger, Todd Fuller, David Griffin, Debby Kaspari, Kiana Koenen, Eric Strauss, Jen Strules, and an anonymous reviewer. Dr. Todd Fuller, a professor in the Department of Natural Resources at University of Massachusetts–Amherst, was especially encouraging and supportive. The enthusiasm and optimism that he brings to his work are infectious, to the great benefit of all who are lucky enough to work with him. Likewise, Dr. Rob Deblinger, deputy director of the Massachusetts Division of Fisheries and Wildlife, has been extraordinarily insightful and supportive. Rob, more than anyone, has created incredible opportunities for me to conduct research in the realm of urban-suburban wildlife and human-wildlife interactions.

Other people contributed to the writing of this book without really knowing it, mostly by sharing a part of their lives with me, by engaging in all manner of conversation that helped shape my ideas and my writing, or by providing inspiration and insight from their work and writing. To start with, I had the unwavering support and love of my parents, Lawrence and Doris DeStefano, to whom I dedicate this book, and the unsuspecting contributions continued with my brothers and sisters, Larry DeStefano, Gerry DeFeo, Susan Copithorne, and David DeStefano, my life-longest friends Dennis LaPointe and Donny White (who is also a first cousin), my high school biology teacher and early mentor George D. Buckley, my colleagues and friends Richard M. DeGraaf, Bill "Wild Bill" Kuvlevsky, Bob Steidl, and Curt Meine, and a large number of colleagues and grad students (especially Dave Wattles, Ken Berger, Jennifer Strules, Luanne Johnson, Kyle McCarthy, Mike Huguenin, and Justin Compton) from the universities of Wisconsin, Idaho, Oregon (Oregon State University), Arizona, and Massachusetts. I also thank Debby Kaspari for creating the beautiful illustrations that show so well in images what I tried to portray in words.

I relied on several references, the scientific literature, and my own experiences in the field as the basis for the parts on coyote behavior, biology, and ecology, but I drew particularly heavily from Gerry Parker's excellent book, *Eastern Coyote: The Story of Its Success* (1995). As is often stated but nonetheless always appropriate to express, the responsibility for the descriptions and conclusions made in this book, as well as any inaccuracies or liberties of interpretation, are my own.

And then there is Ki, my wife, colleague, and friend, who helped me along with every step of the writing and everything else I've gotten myself into since our first conversation under that alligator juniper in the Santa Catalina Mountains. "Thank you" does not nearly say it enough.

Index

Illustrations

by Debby Kaspari